A Fresh Touch of Natural Goodness,

30p

D1436550

A Fresh Touch of Natural Goodness

Milk Marketing Board for Northern Ireland

Published by:
The Milk Marketing Board for Northern Ireland,
456 Antrim Road, Belfast BT15 5GD.

First published 1988

Senior Home Economist
Liz Ritchie, Milk Marketing Board for Northern Ireland.

Printed by:
W. & G. Baird Ltd., Antrim.

Designed by:
Rodney Miller Associates, Belfast.

Food Photography:
Paul Webster, London.

Home Economist: Food Photography
Elaine Bastable.

Location Photography:
Christopher Hill, Belfast.

It is 10 years since the first edition of "A Touch of Natural Goodness" was published. In the intervening years it has become a popular book for cooks throughout Northern Ireland, with many of the recipes becoming firm favourites.

Building on that success, "A Fresh Touch of Natural Goodness" has been published, once again emphasizing that good, natural milk and dairy products can combine to make dishes that are not only simple to prepare and delicious to eat, but also in these days of health awareness, reassuringly nutritious for all the family.

Fashions in cooking change slowly – but there is no doubt that the last ten years have seen great changes in Northern Ireland . . . a more frequent use of herbs and spices, flavoured yogurts and cheeses, and more variety in vegetarian dishes.

So, with these fresh touches in mind, combined with all the traditional methods and ingredients for which Northern Ireland is famous, enjoy trying a few of the exciting new dishes, as well as variations on some of your old favourites.

Either way, good cooking, good eating, and good health!

Liz Ritchie

Senior Home Economist

CONTENTS

Lower Lough Erne, Co. Fermanagh

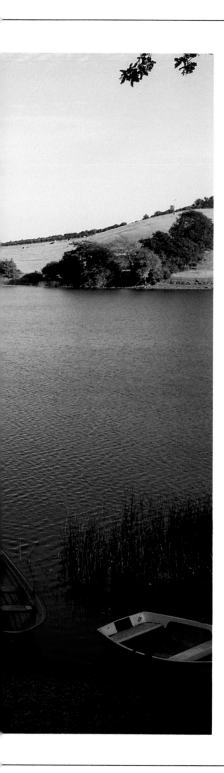

Starters

Whether it is for family or friends, choosing the right starter can be the most important part of a meal. "Well begun is half done" as the proverb says. The starter should take the edge off the appetite and make each person anticipate with pleasure the rest of the meal to come; but it must not be so heavy as to leave you dreading the main course!

Starters should be light and tasty. These recipes have great versatility as they can be easily expanded to make a snack or lunch for the family. To soups you could add some wheaten bread, with butter and a wedge of cheese; and to pâtés, a simple (or not so simple) salad.

Chinese Chicken Soup

225 g (8 oz) uncooked chicken –
sliced

50 g (2 oz) plain flour – seasoned

25 g (1 oz) NI Butter

50 g (2 oz) mushrooms – sliced

300 ml (½ pt) chicken stock

426 ml (¾ pt) NI Milk

1.25 cm (½ in.) root ginger –
grated

10 ml (1 dsp) soya sauce

6–8 spring onions – sliced
lengthwise

100 g (4 oz) bean sprouts

100 g (4 oz) water chestnuts –
optional

Coat chicken in seasoned flour.
Melt butter in a large saucepan
and sauté chicken pieces. Add
mushrooms, and any remaining
flour; then stir in stock, milk,
ginger and soya sauce. Simmer
until chicken is tender. Add
onions, bean sprouts and chestnuts and warm gently. Serve
with prawn crackers.

Tomato and Basil Soup

25 g (1 oz) NI Butter

1 onion – chopped

100 g (4 oz) back bacon – chopped

50 g (2 oz) wholemeal flour

426 ml (¾ pt) NI Milk

150 ml (¼ pt) chicken stock

2 x 397 g (14 oz) tins tomatoes

1 bay leaf

15 ml (1 tbsp) fresh basil –
chopped

pepper

125 ml (4.4 fl oz) fresh NI
Whipping Cream

Melt butter and fry onion and
bacon. Add the flour and cook
for 2 minutes. Gradually add
milk stirring continuously until
sauce cooks and thickens. Add
stock, tomatoes, bay leaf and
basil and simmer for 10 minutes.
Season to taste. Stir in 30 ml (2
tbsp) cream. Remove the bay
leaf and liquidise. Serve with a
swirl of the remaining cream.

Orange and Carrot Soup

25 g (1 oz) NI Butter

1 onion – chopped

450 g (1 lb) carrots – sliced

50 g (2 oz) plain flour

568 ml (1 pt) NI Milk

600 ml (1 pt) chicken stock

pepper

pinch ground nutmeg

2 oranges – rind and juice

Melt butter, add onion and carrots and cook gently without
colouring. Stir in flour and cook
for 1–2 minutes. Gradually add
milk and stock. Season and add
nutmeg. Bring to the boil stirring
constantly, then simmer for
20–30 minutes. Liquidise. Add
orange rind and juice and reheat
but do not boil. Serve with a little
whipped fresh dairy cream and
chopped parsley for decoration.

8

SALT –

You will notice that throughout
this cookery book, salt is omitted
from the majority of recipes.
This is generally because fresh
herbs are used in many of the
recipes to give flavour. If you
wish you can add additional seasoning, sparingly.

Spinach Pâté

300 g (11 oz) pk creamed spinach – frozen

1 clove garlic – crushed

100 g (4 oz) NI Butter – melted

1 sardine

2.5 ml (½ tsp) ground nutmeg

ground pepper

lemon twists

Cook spinach with the garlic. Cool, place in processor along with remaining ingredients and liquidise. Adjust seasoning and spoon into individual pâté dishes. Chill. Garnish with a twist of lemon. Serve immediately on fingers of toast.
NB Best eaten on the day it is made.

Crab Chaussons

215 g (7½ oz) pk frozen puff pastry

1 size 3 egg – beaten

Filling

25 g (1 oz) NI Butter

1 small onion – chopped

100 g (4 oz) mushrooms – sliced

5 ml (1 tsp) tomato purée

30 ml (2 tbsp) white wine

pepper

169 g (6 oz) tin white crabmeat – flaked

Pastry – Roll out thinly and cut into 20 circles with an 8 cm (3 in.) plain cutter. Take each round and roll it in middle to elongate the pastry to an oval.

Filling – Melt butter and sauté onion. Add mushrooms, purée and wine. Simmer for 3–4 minutes. Leave to cool slightly. Season and mix in crabmeat. Place a teaspoon of filling into each pastry piece. Brush edges with beaten egg and press firmly together. Place on an oiled baking tray, reverse way up to help to keep the turnover closed during cooking. Brush top with beaten egg. Bake at 425°F, 220°C, Mark 7 for 15 minutes.

Avocado and Seafood Toss

2 avocados – stoned and peeled

15 ml (1 tbsp) lemon juice

1 small green pepper – deseeded and finely chopped

1 red pepper – deseeded and finely chopped

15 ml (1 tbsp) mayonnaise

75 g (3 oz) white crabmeat

71 ml (⅛ pt) fresh NI Double Cream – whipped

pinch chilli powder

pepper

Mash together flesh of avocados and lemon juice. Add remaining ingredients. Spread on fingers of toast and decorate with lemon wedges and watercress. Alternatively use as a dip.

Sardine Pâté

2 x 120 g (4½ oz) tins sardines in soya oil – drained

25 g (1 oz) shallots – skinned and finely chopped

114 g (4 oz) NI natural Cottage Cheese – sieved

60 ml (4 tbsp) fresh NI Whipping Cream

15 ml (1 tbsp) tomato ketchup

10 ml (1 dsp) lemon juice

pepper

50 g (2 oz) NI Butter – clarified

Gently fry shallots in 5 ml (1 tsp) reserved oil. Mash sardines and mix with shallots, cheese, cream, ketchup, lemon juice, and pepper. Spoon into 570 ml (1 pt) dish or individual pâté dishes and chill to firm. Prepare clarified butter. Cool slightly and spoon over pâté. Return to fridge to set.

To Clarify Butter – Melt 225 g (8 oz) salted butter in a small saucepan over a gentle heat and cook, without stirring, until the butter begins to foam. Continue to cook without browning until the foaming stops. Remove from the heat and allow to stand until the milky deposits have sunk to the bottom, leaving a clear yellow liquid. Strain this through muslin. Makes approximately 150 g (5 oz).

Prawns with Garlic

50 g (2 oz) NI Butter

1 onion – finely chopped

2 cloves garlic – crushed

1 green pepper – cut into strips

450 g (1 lb) peeled prawns or scampi meats

15 ml (1 tbsp) lemon juice

black pepper

Melt butter in a frying pan and gently fry the vegetables. Add the prawns and gently fry for 2–3 minutes (scampi meat 4–5 minutes). Add lemon juice and season. Serve hot.

Stuffed Mushrooms

(not illustrated)

4–6 large open mushrooms

50 g (2 oz) NI Butter – softened

1 large clove garlic – crushed

15 ml (1 tbsp) parsley – chopped

15 ml (1 tbsp) lemon juice

50 g (2 oz) brown breadcrumbs

Wipe mushrooms with clean, damp cloth. Make garlic butter with butter, garlic, parsley and lemon juice. Spread the inside of mushrooms liberally with garlic butter and top with breadcrumbs. Bake at 375°F, 190°C, Mark 5 for 15 minutes.

Scallops with Lime and Ginger Sauce

(not illustrated)

8 large scallops

1 lime – rind and juice

2.5 cm (1 in.) piece fresh ginger – sliced

45 ml (3 tbsp) white port

125 ml (4.4 fl oz) fresh NI Double Cream

15 g (½ oz) NI Butter

white pepper

few shreds of fresh ginger to garnish

Dry the scallops and remove the black thread of the intestines. Reserve a few shreds of lime rind for the garnish and place the remaining rind, with the juice, in a pan with the ginger and the white port. Bring to the boil and cook until the liquid is reduced to 1 tablespoon. Gently heat the cream and add the reduced cooking liquor. Simmer gently for a few minutes. Meanwhile, melt the butter in another pan and fry the scallops for 3–4 minutes on both sides until browned. Season, then remove to 4 warm plates. Pour the cream mixture into the scallop pan, stirring to incorporate the cooking juices. Bring the sauce to the boil, then strain. Spoon around the scallops. Garnish the sauce with the reserved lime rind and shredded ginger.

Avocado with Cheese Dressing

1 avocado – halved and stoned
15 ml (1 tbsp) NI Cheddar Cheese with beer and garlic – grated
5 ml (1 tsp) lemon juice
45 ml (3 tbsp) NI natural Yogurt
30 ml (2 tbsp) dry roasted peanuts – coarsely chopped

Scoop flesh out of avocado and finely chop. Blend with cheese and lemon juice to make a paste. Fold in yogurt. Spoon mixture into avocado shells. Chill. Sprinkle with peanuts just before serving.

Egg and Caviare Slice

50 g (2 oz) NI Butter
5 size 3 eggs – hard-boiled and chopped
2 spring onions – chopped
2 x 150 ml (5.3 oz) NI Soured Cream
40 ml (4 dsp) caviare (lump fish)

Cream butter and eggs together or liquidise to form a soft paste and use to cover the base of a lined 20 cm (8 in.) cake tin. Freeze until firm. Mix the onions and soured cream together and spread on top of egg paste. Freeze until firm – approximately half an hour. Remove from tin, and spoon caviare on top just before serving. Cut into 8 portions and serve on individual plates with toast, garnished with lettuce, lemon and tomato slices.

Tarragon and Seafood Toss

1 ripe avocado – peeled and stoned
30 ml (2 tbsp) lemon juice
100 g (4 oz) smoked salmon – cut into strips
100 g (4 oz) prawns – peeled
15 ml (1 tbsp) fresh tarragon – chopped
150 ml (5.3 oz) NI Soured Cream
62 g (2.2 oz) NI natural Yogurt
15 ml (1 tbsp) mayonnaise
pepper and paprika pepper
1 head chicory

Cut avocado into small chunks, toss in lemon juice and mix with smoked salmon and prawns. Mix the tarragon, soured cream, yogurt and mayonnaise together and season with pepper and paprika pepper. Toss the avocado, smoked salmon and prawn mixture gently in the dressing. Taste and adjust the seasoning. Spoon onto serving plates, sprinkle with paprika pepper and serve with chicory.

Mushrooms in Cream

25 g (1 oz) NI Butter
1 onion – chopped
450 g (1 lb) button mushrooms
150 ml (5.3 oz) NI Soured Cream
30 ml (2 tbsp) parsley – chopped
pepper

Melt butter and fry onion until transparent, add mushrooms and cook for 3–4 minutes until tender. (If they make a lot of liquid, boil vigorously for a minute or two to evaporate it). Reduce heat, stir in soured cream, pepper and heat through gently (do not boil). Spoon into a warmed serving dish or individual dishes and sprinkle with parsley.

Minnowburn, Edenderry, Co. Antrim

Salads

Gone are the days when a salad meant a few limp lettuce leaves garnished with a slice of tomato and a hard-boiled egg. With the huge range of herbs, spices and vegetables now available it is easy to be more adventurous. Some of these recipes use ingredients you may not have dreamed of putting in a salad a few years ago.

Salads are flexible: some, such as those with fish or chicken in the recipes, can be a meal in themselves, eaten with bread or potatoes. Others are perfect accompaniments to main courses, as an alternative to the traditional "two veg". Either way, they make a healthy meal, full of nutrition and, for those who care about such things, wonderfully non-fattening.

Herby Potatoes

675 g (1½ lb) small new potatoes

50 g (2 oz) NI Butter

30 ml (2 tbsp) fresh mixed herbs (parsley, chives, tarragon)

black pepper

Cook potatoes until just tender. Drain. Cream butter with fresh herbs and pepper. Place potatoes in serving dish and dot with butter mixture.

Coleslaw with Caraway

(not illustrated)

1 large white cabbage – cored and shredded

1 onion – finely chopped

1 green pepper – deseeded and finely chopped

2.5 ml (½ tsp) lemon juice

15 ml (1 tbsp) caraway seeds

Dressing

175 ml (6 fl oz) fresh NI Double Cream – lightly whipped

90 ml (3 oz) NI Soured Cream

15 ml (1 tbsp) French mustard

45 ml (3 tbsp) lemon juice

15 ml (1 tbsp) sugar

2.5 ml (½ tsp) salt

pinch white pepper

In a large bowl, toss together cabbage, onion, pepper and lemon juice. In another bowl blend together the ingredients for the dressing. Pour dressing over the cabbage mixture and stir well. Add the caraway seeds and mix through. Chill and serve cold.

Chicory and Mushroom Salad

(not illustrated)

1 head chicory

225 g (8 oz) button mushrooms – sliced

298 g (10½ oz) tin mandarin oranges (in natural juice) – drained

50 g (2 oz) nuts – chopped

black pepper

125 g (4.4 oz) NI natural Yogurt

Use chicory to line salad bowl. Combine mushrooms, oranges, nuts and pepper together. Toss in yogurt. Place in salad bowl and garnish with watercress.

Cress and Melon Salad

1 bunch watercress – trimmed

4 medium bananas – thinly sliced

½ lemon – juice

45 ml (3 tbsp) mayonnaise

150 ml (5.3 oz) NI Soured Cream

45 ml (3 tbsp) parsley – chopped

pepper

1 medium cantaloupe melon – diced

50 g (2 oz) walnuts – chopped

Arrange watercress round edge of serving dish. Toss bananas in lemon juice. Blend mayonnaise, cream and parsley together, fold in bananas, melon and walnuts. Season. Place in dish, sprinkle with paprika pepper and chill for ½ hour before serving.

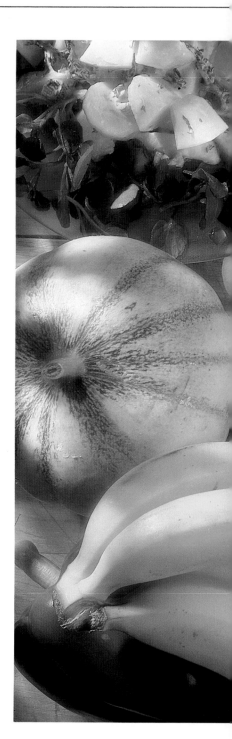

Smoked Fish and Pasta Salad

125 g (4.4 oz) NI natural Yogurt
60 ml (4 tbsp) mayonnaise
15–30 ml (1–2 tbsp) horseradish sauce
pepper
15 ml (1 tbsp) lemon juice
225 g (8 oz) pasta bows – cooked
325 g (12 oz) frozen smoked kipper fillets – cooked and flaked
3 sticks celery – thinly sliced
4 spring onions – sliced

Mix the yogurt, mayonnaise, horseradish sauce, pepper and lemon juice together. Stir in the pasta, fish, celery and spring onions. Season. Sprinkle with a little paprika and garnish with lemon wedges.

Curried Grapefruit Salad

2 grapefruit – peel and segment
1 sweetie or pink grapefruit – peel and segment
450–675 g (1–1½ lb) cooked turkey/chicken – diced
3–5 celery sticks – chopped
3 large tomatoes – quartered
1 green pepper – deseeded and chopped

Dressing

150 ml (¼ pt) mayonnaise
125 g (4.4 oz) NI natural Yogurt
10 ml (1 dsp) curry powder

Place grapefruit and sweetie segments plus their juice in a bowl and mix with meat, celery, tomatoes and green pepper.

Dressing – Mix ingredients together and then toss salad ingredients in it. Chill until required and serve on a bed of crisp lettuce. Garnish with pepper rings.

Cucumber Celery Potatoes

675 g (1½ lb) small new potatoes
4 sticks celery – diced
½ cucumber – diced
125 g (4.4 oz) NI natural Yogurt
10 ml (1 dsp) fresh mint – chopped
pepper

Cook potatoes until just tender. Drain and cool and place in a serving dish. In a bowl mix together celery, cucumber, yogurt, mint and pepper. Spoon over potatoes. Garnish with celery leaves.

Tuna Bean Salad

75 g (3 oz) green pasta shells – cooked and drained

¼ cucumber – diced

198 g (7 oz) tin tuna fish (in brine) – drained

213 g (7.51 oz) tin kidney beans – drained

Dressing

125 g (4.4 oz) NI natural Yogurt

45 ml (3 tbsp) NI Milk

10 ml (1 dsp) lemon juice

15 ml (1 tbsp) tomato ketchup

pepper

Mix the dressing ingredients together. Add the salad ingredients and toss together. Serve on a bed of lettuce.

Herring Salad

4 herrings – boned

1 onion – thinly sliced

5 ml (1 tsp) fresh tarragon – chopped

6 peppercorns

150 ml (¼ pt) fish or chicken stock

150 ml (¼ pt) wine vinegar

125 g (4.4 oz) NI natural Yogurt

1 red or green eating apple – chopped

lemon juice.

Roll herrings and secure fish with cocktail sticks, place in an ovenproof dish and cover with onion, seasonings and liquids. Poach at 325°F, 170°C, Mark 3 for 30 minutes. Cool and chill. Drain the fish, reserving the liquid and arrange on a serving dish. Blend yogurt and 30 ml (2 tbsp) fish stock together and spoon over fish. Garnish with apple pieces tossed in lemon juice.

Spiced Chicken Salad

125 g (4.4 oz) NI natural Yogurt

pepper

2.5 ml (½ tsp) curry powder

pinch ground ginger

1 small onion – chopped

½ green pepper – chopped

2 sticks celery – chopped

50 g (2 oz) black grapes – halved and deseeded

225 g (8 oz) chicken – cooked and diced

50 g (2 oz) all-bran cereal

Place yogurt in a bowl and fold in remaining ingredients. Cover with cling film and chill thoroughly. Serve with leaves of lettuce and garnish with grapes.

The Mournes, Co. Down

Main Courses & Snacks

A clutch of simple basic ingredients can be transformed into a feast with a spoonful of herbs or spices, or the inclusion of a flavoursome smooth sauce. More mature cooks have learnt a thing or two in this respect from daughters and even grand-daughters!

Most menfolk are slower to adjust to what they call "fancy food" such as the Chicken Tikka, or Moussaka, which are included in this section. The solution is to serve them up without comment – you will be surprised how cosmopolitan they become. They will even accept pasta instead of potatoes, if it is well presented.

Herbs

A culinary herb is any herbaceous plant (one that dies in winter) that adds flavour to food. Herbs are invaluable in cooking as they help to enhance the flavour, (even in the most basic dishes) and also help to reduce the amount of salt used in cooking.

Fresh herbs are readily available now and are also easy to grow both inside and outside. About two-thirds of herbs die completely or to ground level in autumn and therefore need to be preserved.

To Preserve herbs

1. Place the sprigs in small jars, dampen with fresh lemon juice and store in the refrigerator.
2. To freeze – snip herbs with scissors, spoon them into ice-cube containers, cover with cold water and fast freeze. The ice-cubes can then be stored in polythene bags. Six months storage time.
3. To dry – tie in small bundles and hang in a warm place for 2–3 weeks until they become brittle, or place on a drying tray in an airing cupboard or a very cool oven, or in a microwave oven. Dried herbs should be stored in small, clean, dry, glass jars with tight fitting lids. Store in a cool, dark, dry place. They last for approximately one year and if they smell dusty, they should be discarded.

When cooking with herbs, remember they should be used sparingly so that they complement different ingredients in the dish rather than dominating it. A guide is – approximately 5 ml (1 tsp) dried herbs, 15 ml (1 tbsp) fresh herbs and slightly more than 15 ml (1 tbsp) frozen herbs for 4 people.

Some herbs are delicate and should be added towards the end of the cooking time eg basil and tarragon, whereas others which are more robust need a longer cooking time eg bayleaf, marjoram and thyme. Some herbs are better added to a dish at the end of the cooking time, in order to retain their colour eg parsley and chives.

Herbs are normally chopped or pounded in order to release their flavouring oils. If colour retention is important it is best to use a stainless steel knife.

Different herbs have become associated with different foods – certainly use this as a guide but do experiment for yourself.

The following list gives a guide to the types of herbs used in these recipes.

Parsley

Parsley used to be called the "Herb of Health", and was very popular in ancient Rome. It is the stalks rather than the leaves which add a lovely flavour to almost any savoury dish. In addition parsley is an attractive garnish.

Bay

This is an evergreen tree. The fresh leaves are the nicest and Tom Stobard, a food writer once said, "no self-respecting European kitchen, cooks without them". It gives a lovely flavour to oily fish, pork, veal, boiled bacon, pâtés, soups, stews, custards and milk puddings.

Chives

They belong to the same family as garlic, shallots and leeks and impart a delicate onion flavour to dishes. Use with eggs, fish, poultry, cream cheese, salads and in savoury sauces. Also suitable as a garnish.

Garlic

This is a dried herb and a member of the onion family. The bulb is easily broken into "cloves" and after the papery skin is removed, is ready for use. It adds zest to vegetables, meat, poultry, game and fish. For a strong flavour, mash it to a purée with a pinch of salt or for a mild flavour, rub the peeled clove around the inside of the dish.

Marjoram

It is warm and sweet-flavoured and a traditional ingredient in mixed herbs together with thyme and sage. It is ideal with meat, strongly flavoured oily fish, grilled mushrooms, tomato dishes, eggs, cheese and vegetables.

Mint

The leaves contain menthol which imparts its characteristic taste. A little sugar added to the mint when chopping helps draw out the flavour. It is ideal in herb butters, stuffings, new potatoes, salads, and lamb roasted on a bed of mint leaves, is delicious. In addition it enhances the flavour of ice-cream, sorbets, custards and fruit salad and it is a lovely garnish for cold drinks.

There are several varieties of mint e.g. spearmint, peppermint and apple mint.

Oregano

Oregano is similar to the British plant, "wild marjoram", and dries very well. It keeps for about 3 years in the dried form. It is widely used in Italian cookery eg pizzas and lasagne.

Sauces

Sauces have been in widespread use since the Middle Ages. It is often said that "A good sauce should have a flavour and be so discreetly blended that on tasting it, you feel it might be eaten by itself".

Today sauces are generally used to add flavour, colour and moisture to dishes. The consistency can be altered by varying the proportions of butter and plain flour or cornflour to the liquid. The secret in making a perfect sauce lies in giving it your full attention for the few minutes it takes to prepare it. In this book it is a "Coating White Sauce" that is used. Here is a fool-proof way to make it.

All-in-one Method

Place in a saucepan 25 g (1 oz) NI Butter, 25 g (1 oz) plain flour or cornflour and 284 ml (½ pt) NI Milk. Heat, whisking continuously until the sauce thickens and is cooked. Season.

Blender/Food Processor Method

Use ingredients in the same quantities as above. Place the ingredients in the machine and blend until smooth. Pour into a saucepan and bring to the boil, stirring, until the sauce thickens.

Variations

For the following sauces make 284 ml (½ pt) white coating sauce.

1. *Cheese Sauce*

Remove from heat and stir in 75 g (3 oz) NI grated Cheddar Cheese, until melted. Add a pinch of dry mustard and pepper.

2. *Parsley or Herb Sauce*

After seasoning, stir in 15–30 ml (1-2 tbsp) finely chopped fresh parsley or fresh herb of choice.

3. *Tomato Sauce*

Add 30 ml (2 tbsp) tomato purée to the basic white sauce.

4. *White Wine Sauce*

Place half a bottle of white wine into a saucepan with 4 peppercorns. Reduce this over a low heat to about 60 ml (4 tbsp). Strain into the basic white sauce when cool and beat well.

Bacon Pasta

175g (6 oz) green or white tagliatelle pasta

5 rashers smoked back bacon – chopped

1 onion – thinly sliced

15 g (½ oz) cornflour

2 x 125 g (4.4 oz) NI natural Yogurt

2 size 3 eggs – beaten

pepper

75 g (3 oz) NI Cheddar Cheese – grated

Cook pasta in boiling salted water until tender. Drain and keep warm in a casserole dish. Fry bacon and onion until soft. Mix cornflour with a little of measured yogurt. In a saucepan mix remainder of yogurt and eggs together, heat and add blended cornflour. Cook for a few minutes stirring continuously. Season and stir in bacon and onion. Pour over pasta. Sprinkle with cheese and brown under the grill. Serve immediately.

Crispy Tuna Pie

198 g (7 oz) tin tuna fish – in oil

15 g (½ oz) NI Butter

20 g (¾ oz) cornflour

284 ml (½ pt) NI Milk

pepper

Topping

75 g (3 oz) plain flour

40 g (1½ oz) NI Butter

50 g (2 oz) NI Cheddar Cheese – grated

25 g (1 oz) plain potato crisps – crushed

pepper

Melt butter with 30 ml (2 tbsp) tuna fish oil. Add cornflour and cook for one minute. Add milk, bring to boil , remove from heat and add seasoning and tuna. Pour into oiled casserole dish.

Topping – Rub butter into flour and mix in cheese, crisps and seasoning. Sprinkle evenly over mixture. Bake at 375°F, 190°C, Mark 5 for 25–30 minutes. Garnish with a sprig of parsley.

Moussaka

1 large aubergine

5 ml (1 tsp) salt

25 g (1 oz) NI Butter

15 ml (1 tbsp) oil

450 g (1 lb) minced beef

1 large onion – chopped

1 clove garlic – crushed

213 g (7 ½ oz) tin tomatoes

pepper

Sauce

227 g (8 oz) NI natural Cottage Cheese – sieved

1 size 3 egg – beaten

25 g (1 oz) NI Cheddar Cheese – grated

Slice aubergine thinly, spread them on a tray and sprinkle with salt. Leave for a few hours, pour off liquid, run under cold water, dry well and fry in butter and oil. Brown beef in its own fat, add onion and garlic and fry for a few minutes. Stir in tomatoes and pepper and cook for 10–15 minutes. Oil an ovenproof dish and place half aubergines in the bottom, cover with half of beef mixture. Repeat layers.

Sauce – Beat cottage cheese and egg together and pour over Moussaka. Top with cheese. Bake at 350°F, 180°C, Mark 4 for 25–30 minutes.

Harvest Bake

450 g (1 lb) minced beef
25 g (1 oz) plain flour
300 ml (½ pt) beef stock
15 ml (1 tbsp) fresh mixed herbs
pepper
30 ml (2 tbsp) tomato purée
100 g (4 oz) leeks – washed and sliced
175 g (6 oz) cauliflower – divided into small florets
100 g (4 oz) carrots – finely diced
450 g (1 lb) potatoes – cooked and sliced

Topping

10 ml (1 dsp) cornflour
2 x 125 g (4.4 oz) NI natural Yogurt
10 ml (1 dsp) fresh mixed herbs
75 g (3 oz) NI Cheddar Cheese – grated

Brown beef in its own fat and drain off any excess. Stir in flour. Gradually blend in stock. Bring to the boil and add herbs, pepper, purée, leeks, cauliflower and carrots. Cover and simmer for 15 minutes, stirring occasionally.
Place in deep ovenproof dish. Cover with sliced potatoes.

Topping – Place cornflour in bowl. Gradually blend in yogurt. Stir in herbs. Pour over potatoes. Top with cheese. Bake at 375°F, 190°C, Mark 5 for 35–45 minutes.

Pasta Shepherd's Pie
(not illustrated)

1 onion – sliced
450 g (1 lb) minced beef
1 clove garlic – crushed
pepper
15 ml (1 tbsp) tomato purée
397 g (14 oz) tin tomatoes
15 ml (1 tbsp) fresh mixed herbs

Topping

2 x 125 g (4.4 oz) NI natural Yogurt
2 size 3 eggs – beaten
75 g (3 oz) NI Cheddar Cheese – grated
175 g (6 oz) short-cut macaroni – cooked

Brown beef in its own fat and drain off any excess. Add onion, garlic, pepper, purée, tomatoes and herbs. Simmer for 20 minutes. Place meat mixture in an ovenproof dish.

Topping – Mix together yogurt, eggs, 50 g (2 oz) cheese and the macaroni. Pour evenly over the meat mixture. Sprinkle with the remaining cheese. Bake at 375°F, 190°C, Mark 5 for 20–30 minutes.

Courgette and Potato Casserole
(not illustrated)

450 g (1 lb) minced beef
1 onion – chopped
1 clove garlic – crushed
45 ml (3 tbsp) tomato purée
2.5 ml (½ tsp) ground allspice
5 ml (1 tsp) fresh oregano
pepper
150 ml (¼ pt) beef stock
25 g (1 oz) NI Butter
15 ml (1 tbsp) oil
450 g (1 lb) courgettes – sliced
450 g (1 lb) potatoes – cooked and sliced

Cheese Sauce

25 g (1 oz) NI Butter
25 g (1 oz) plain flour
284 ml (½ pt) NI Milk
75 g (3 oz) NI Cheddar Cheese – grated
pinch mustard
pepper

Brown beef in its own fat and drain off any excess. Add onion and garlic and cook for a further few minutes. Add purée, allspice, oregano, pepper and stock, cover and simmer for 5 to 10 minutes. Cook courgettes in butter and oil until soft.

Sauce – Make by all-in-one method. Remove from the heat, add half of cheese, mustard and pepper. Layer meat mixture, courgettes and potatoes in an ovenproof dish. Pour the sauce over the top and sprinkle with the remaining cheese. Bake at 375°F, 190°C, Mark 5 for 25–30 minutes.

Chicken Tikka

325 g (12 oz) chicken breast – skinned

30 ml (2 tbsp) lemon juice

2 x 125 g (4.4 oz) NI natural Yogurt

1 onion – chopped

5 ml (1 tsp) fresh ginger – finely chopped

½ green chilli – deseeded and chopped

2.5 ml (½ tsp) ground turmeric

5 ml (1 tsp) garam masala

Sauce

50 g (2 oz) NI Butter

10 ml (1 dsp) fresh coriander – finely chopped

60 ml (4 tbsp) fresh NI Double Cream

pinch cayenne pepper

lettuce – shredded

Cut the chicken into medium-sized chunks and sprinkle with lemon juice. Mix yogurt with the onion, ginger, chilli and spices. Liquidise or process until smooth. Pour the mixture over the chicken, mix well, then cover and leave to marinate overnight. When ready to serve, set the oven at the highest setting. Remove the chicken from the marinade (reserving the liquid) and arrange the chunks in a single layer in a shallow ovenproof dish. Cook for 10–15 minutes until tender.

Sauce – Melt butter and add the reserved marinade. Stir in the coriander, cream and cayenne and heat gently. Arrange lettuce on a serving plate. Place chicken pieces on top and spoon over the sauce. Serve the dish with fingers of warm pitta bread or a bowl of steamed rice.

Apricot Chicken Curry

1 onion – chopped

25 g (1 oz) NI Butter – melted

10 ml (1 dsp) brown sugar

15 ml (1 tbsp) lemon juice

15 ml (1 tbsp) curry powder

15 ml (1 tbsp) tomato puree

150 ml (¼ pt) red wine

1 bay leaf

seasoning

450 g (1 lb) large chicken cubes – cooked

1 small tin apricots – drained and puréed

150 ml (¼ pt) mayonnaise

125 ml (4.4 fl oz) fresh NI Double Cream

rice

Cook onion in butter. Stir in sugar, lemon juice, curry powder, purée, wine, bay leaf and seasoning. Mix well. Stir in chicken, apricot purée, mayonnaise and cream. Heat through but do not boil. Serve on a bed of rice. Garnish with a fresh bay leaf.

Curry

40 g (1½ oz) NI Butter

2 onions – chopped

2 cloves garlic – crushed

5 ml (1 tsp) salt

5 ml (1 tsp) chilli powder

5 ml (1 tsp) ground black pepper

5 ml (1 tsp) ground cumin

5 ml (1 tsp) garam masala

2.5 ml (½ tsp) nutmeg

10 ml (1 dsp) paprika pepper

5 ml (1 tsp) turmeric

25 g (1 oz) fresh root ginger – peeled and grated

5 ml (1 tsp) cornflour

125 ml (4.4 fl oz) fresh NI Whipping Cream

2 x 125 g (4.4 oz) NI natural Yogurt

100 g (4 oz) unsalted cashew nuts

900 g (2 lb) large chicken or pork cubes – cooked

Melt butter in a large pan, add onions and garlic and cook until lightly browned. Add the spices and cook, for 10 minutes. Mix cornflour with a little cream to a smooth paste and add to sauce, stirring continuously. Stir in remainder of cream, yogurt and nuts. Heat through but do not boil. Add chicken or pork, cover and simmer for 40–50 minutes. Garnish with a sprig of coriander and serve with poppadums.

Cyprus Chicken

25 g (1 oz) NI Butter

30 ml (2 tbsp) oil

100 g (4 oz) rice

1 orange – rind and juice

15 ml (1 tbsp) wine vinegar

30 ml (2 tbsp) white wine

1 green pepper – diced

300 ml (½ pt) chicken stock

450 g (1 lb) cooked chicken – cubed

71 ml (⅛ pt) fresh NI Double Cream

5 ml (1 tsp) fresh mixed herbs

pepper

50 g (2 oz) flaked almonds – toasted

Melt butter and oil together in a frying pan. Fry the rice for 15 minutes. Add orange juice, vinegar, wine, stock, green pepper and chicken. Cook until rice is tender. Mix together cream, herbs, orange rind and pepper and add to rice mixture. Heat through but do not boil. Garnish with flaked almonds and a sprig of parsley.

Chicken and Bacon Casserole

6 chicken thighs – skinned

6 rashers rindless back bacon

20 g (¾ oz) NI Butter

1 onion – chopped

black pepper

5 ml (1 tsp) fresh tarragon – chopped

600 ml (1 pt) chicken stock

100 g (4 oz) mushrooms – sliced

25 g (1 oz) cornflour

125 ml (4.4 fl oz) fresh NI Double Cream

Wrap each chicken thigh with a rasher of bacon. Melt butter in large pan and cook onion until soft, add chicken joints and brown. Add stock, tarragon and seasoning. Cover the pan and simmer for 20 minutes. Add mushrooms and cook for a further 30 minutes. Remove chicken joints and keep warm. Stir cornflour into cream to make a smooth paste and stir into juices. Cook over a low heat to thicken the sauce. Pour sauce over chicken joints. Serve with new potatoes and carrots.

Chicken Divan

225 g (8 oz) broccoli – cooked

50 g (2 oz) NI Cheddar Cheese – grated

325 g (12 oz) cooked chicken – chopped

Sauce

25 g (1 oz) NI Butter

25 g (1 oz) plain flour

284 ml (½ pt) NI Milk

1 chicken stock cube

ground black pepper

125 ml (4.4 fl oz) fresh NI Whipping Cream

30 ml (2 tbsp) dry sherry

1 size 3 egg yolk

Arrange broccoli in 1 litre (1¾ pt) ovenproof dish. Sprinkle with half of cheese. Arrange chicken on top of broccoli.

Sauce – Make by the all-in-one method. Add stock cube and pepper and bring to boil and simmer for a couple of minutes. Stir in cream. Bring just to boiling point and remove from heat. Beat in sherry and egg yolk. Pour sauce over and sprinkle with remaining cheese. Bake at 350°F, 180°C, Mark 4 for 30 minutes. Serve with pasta and courgettes.

NB Chicken can be replaced by turkey.

Prawn and Vegetable Pasta

175 g (6 oz) pasta shells

15 ml (1 tbsp) oil

25 g (1 oz) NI Butter

4 sticks celery – chopped

Sauce

40 g (1½ oz) NI Butter

40 g (1½ oz) plain flour

568 ml (1 pt) NI Milk

198 g (7 oz) tin sweetcorn – drained

100 g (4 oz) prawns

100 g (4 oz) NI Cheddar Cheese – grated

pepper

pinch mustard

chives – chopped

Cook pasta in boiling water and oil for 20 minutes. Drain and toss in butter and place in oiled ovenproof dish. Parboil celery for 10 minutes. Drain.

Sauce – Make up by the all-in-one method. Remove from the heat and add sweetcorn, prawns, cheese, pepper, mustard and celery. Pour the sauce over the pasta and cook at 375°F, 190°C, Mark 5 for 30 minutes. Sprinkle with chives before serving.

Plaice with Herb Butter

100 g (4 oz) NI Butter

10 ml (1 dsp) fresh mixed herbs

5 ml (1 tsp) lemon juice

black pepper

8 plaice fillets

Cream together butter, herbs, lemon juice and seasoning. Place on a piece of greaseproof paper and roll into a sausage shape. Refrigerate until firm. Grill or fry fish, turning once and place on a hot serving dish. Slice the butter into rounds and place on the fish. Garnish with watercress.

Haddock with Dill Sauce

675 g (1½ lbs) haddock fillets – skinned

284 ml (½ pt) NI Milk

5 ml (1 tsp) fresh dill

black pepper

Sauce

25 g (1 oz) NI Butter

25 g (1 oz) plain flour

1 hard-boiled egg – chopped

Cut haddock into 4 portions, place in a saucepan and pour milk over. Add dill and seasonings and poach gently for 6–8 minutes. Drain fish and keep hot.

Sauce – Make by the all-in-one method, using the reserved milk from the fish. Season as necessary. Stir in the hard-boiled egg. Place fish on serving dish and pour sauce over. Garnish with fresh dill.

Haddock and Potato Cheesecake

Base

100 g (4 oz) self-raising flour

25 g (1 oz) NI Butter

10 ml (1 dsp) fresh mixed herbs

45 ml (3 tbsp) NI Milk

Filling

227 g (8 oz) NI natural Cottage Cheese – sieved

75 g (3 oz) plain flour – seasoned

150 ml (5.3 oz) NI Soured Cream

3 size 3 eggs – separated

175 g (6 oz) smoked haddock – cooked and flaked

75 g (3 oz) NI Cheddar Cheese – grated

2 medium potatoes – cooked and sliced

Base – Rub butter into dry ingredients. Bind together with milk to form an elastic dough. Roll out into a 22 cm (9 in.) circle and use to line a lightly oiled loose-bottomed 20 cm (8 in.) cake tin.

Filling – Blend cottage cheese, flour, soured cream and egg yolks together. Fold in haddock and cheese. Whisk the egg whites until stiff and fold into the mixture. Pour cheese mixture onto the dough and arrange the sliced potatoes on top. Bake at 325°C, 170°C, Mark 3 for approximately 1¼ hours. Serve hot with crisp green salad.

Kedgeree Special

275 g (10 oz) wholegrain rice – rinsed

675 g (1½ lbs) smoked cod

5 ml (1 tsp) black peppercorns

1 bay leaf

1 slice onion

2 green peppers – cored and sliced

50 g (2 oz) NI Butter

30 ml (2 tbsp) oil

1 large onion – thinly sliced

100 g (4 oz) peanuts

50 g (2 oz) raisins

10 ml (1 dsp) curry powder

5 ml (1 tsp) ground turmeric

150 ml (5.3 oz) NI Soured Cream

Cook the rice in boiling, lightly salted water for about 45 minutes until tender. Drain. In a saucepan place fish, peppercorns, bay leaf and onion slice. Cover with cold water and bring to the boil. Simmer gently for 2 minutes. Drain the fish and skin. Remove any bones and flake. Heat butter and oil in a large frying pan and cook peppers and onion until onion is soft. Mix in the rice, fish, nuts, raisins, curry powder and turmeric and stir well until heated right through. Stir in three quarters of the soured cream and heat through – do not boil. Serve immediately topped with remaining soured cream and garnish with lemon slices.

Celery and Courgette Potato Pie

450 g (1 lb) celery – chopped

675 g (1½ lb) potatoes – peeled, sliced and cooked

125 g (4.4 oz) NI natural Yogurt

pepper

900 g (2 lb) whiting – filleted

284 ml (½ pt) NI Milk

1 bay leaf

peppercorns

25 g (1 oz) NI Butter

100 g (4 oz) courgettes – sliced

75 g (3 oz) button mushrooms – sliced

50 g (2 oz) plain flour

fresh dill or parsley – chopped

Boil celery. Drain. Place fish in saucepan, pour milk over, add bay leaf and peppercorns, cover and simmer for 10 minutes or until cooked. Strain the liquid and reserve. Flake fish, discarding any skin and bones. Melt butter, add courgettes and mushrooms and cook for 1–2 minutes. Blend in flour and cook for a further minute. Stir in reserved liquid, bring to the boil and boil for one minute. Add fish, pepper and dill or parsley. Mix celery and yogurt together. Layer fish, celery mixture, and potatoes. Bake at 400°F, 200°C, Mark 6 for 25 minutes.

Sea Food Crumble

225 g (8 oz) smoked haddock – cubed

225 g (8 oz) cod – cubed

1 bay leaf

1 onion – chopped

100 g (4 oz) cooked peeled prawns

284 ml (½ pt) NI Milk

25 g (1 oz) NI Butter

25 g (1 oz) plain flour

1.25 ml (¼ tsp) grated nutmeg

black pepper

30 ml (2 tbsp) parsley – chopped

100 g (4 oz) NI Cheddar Cheese – grated

75 g (3 oz) wholemeal breadcrumbs

Poach the haddock and cod with onion and bay leaf in the milk for about 3 minutes. Lift the fish and onion out and place into a shallow ovenproof dish (discard bay leaf). Sprinkle prawns over. Make sauce by the all-in-one method, using the reserved milk. Season with nutmeg and pepper, then add parsley. Remove from heat and stir in half of the cheese. Pour over fish. Mix remainder of cheese with breadcrumbs and spoon over fish. Bake at 375°F, 190°C, Mark 5 for 20 minutes until crisp and golden.

Broccoli Prawn Pie

450 g (1 lb) cod – cubed

100 g (4 oz) peeled prawns

50 g (2 oz) mushrooms – sliced

295 g (10.4 oz) tin Campbells gourmet cream of broccoli soup or cream of asparagus soup

1 lemon – rind and juice

142 ml (¼ pt) NI Milk

50 g (2 oz) NI Cheddar Cheese – grated

Place fish and mushrooms in an ovenproof dish. Mix together soup, rind and juice of lemon, and milk and pour over the fish mixture. Sprinkle cheese over and bake at 375°F, 190°C, Mark 5 for 25 minutes. Garnish with chopped parsley.

Annalong, Co. Down.

Vegetarian

Whether from principle, for health, or even for economic reasons, there is a growing interest in preparing and eating non-meat meals. The abundance of good fresh vegetables, readily available in Northern Ireland all the year round, makes these recipes easy to include in any culinary planning.

Vegetable Lasagne

9 sheets pre-cooked plain, green or wholemeal lasagne

Ratatouille

1 large aubergine – sliced

50 g (2 oz) NI Butter – melted

30 ml (2 tbsp) oil

1 large onion – sliced

2 cloves garlic – crushed

1 red pepper – sliced

1 green pepper – sliced

225 g (8 oz) courgettes – sliced

225 g (8 oz) tomatoes – skinned and sliced

salt and pepper

Sauce

50 g (2 oz) NI Butter

50 g (2 oz) plain flour

426 ml (¾ pt) NI Milk

250 ml (8.8 fl oz) fresh NI Whipping Cream

225 g (8 oz) NI Cheddar Cheese – grated

pepper

Ratatouille – Sprinkle aubergines with salt and leave aside for half an hour. Rinse, drain and thoroughly dry. Fry onion and garlic in butter and oil, add aubergines, peppers, courgettes and tomatoes. Season. Simmer gently for 10–15 minutes.

Sauce – Make sauce by the all-in-one method. Add cream and cook for a further minute. Remove from heat and beat in 175 g (6 oz) cheese and season. Arrange layers of sauce, lasagne and ratatouille in shallow ovenproof dish, starting and finishing with sauce. Sprinkle with remaining cheese and bake at 375°F, 190°C, Mark 5 for 30–35 minutes.

Aubergine Casserole

450 g (1 lb) aubergines – sliced

5 ml (1 tsp) salt

450 g (1 lb) leeks – sliced

50 g (2 oz) NI Butter

30 ml (2 tbsp) cooking oil

2 red peppers – sliced

175 g (6 oz) NI Cheddar Cheese – grated

125 g (4.4 oz) NI natural Yogurt

black pepper

15 ml (1 tbsp) fresh oregano

Sprinkle aubergine slices with salt and leave for a few hours. Pour off liquid, rinse and dry. Fry aubergines in half the butter and oil. Drain well. Cook leeks in remaining butter and oil for one minute, remove and cook three-quarters of pepper slices for one minute. Put half aubergine slices in a shallow ovenproof dish, cover with half the leeks, one-third of the cheese and half of yogurt. Season. Repeat layers. Form a ring of remaining peppers on top, sprinkle remaining cheese and oregano on top. Bake at 425°F, 220°C, Mark 7 for 20 minutes.

Nutty Potato Nests

5 potatoes – cooked and peeled

25 g (1 oz) NI Butter

1 size 3 egg yolk

114 g (4 oz) NI natural Cottage Cheese

30 ml (2 tbsp) NI natural Yogurt

¼ onion – finely chopped

50 g (2 oz) hazelnuts – finely chopped

2 tomatoes – halved

Mash potatoes with egg yolk and butter. When cool, place in a forcing bag and pipe in 4 nest shapes onto an oiled baking tray. Bake at 375°F, 190°C, Mark 5 for 15 minutes until golden brown. Remove and place on serving dish and keep hot. Fill nests with mixture of cottage cheese, yogurt and onion. Decorate with nuts and serve with half a tomato.

Macaroni Bake (not illustrated)

225 g (8 oz) macaroni – cooked

225 g (8 oz) mixed green vegetables (peas, green beans etc)

198 g (8 oz) tin sweetcorn – drained

4 size 3 eggs – hard-boiled and chopped

Sauce

40g (1½ oz) NI Butter

40 g (1½ oz) plain flour

426 ml (¾ pt) NI Milk

pepper

25 g (1 oz) plain potato crisps – crushed

50 g (2 oz) NI Cheddar Cheese – grated

Combine macaroni with vegetables and eggs and place in an ovenproof dish.

Sauce – Make by the all-in-one method. Season. Pour over macaroni and vegetables and sprinkle over crisps and cheese. Bake at 400°F, 200°C, Mark 6 for 25 minutes.

44

Bean and Broccoli Lasagne *(not illustrated)*

4 sheets fresh lasagne – plain, green or wholemeal

Bean Sauce

25 g (1 oz) NI Butter

5 ml (1 tsp) oil

1 onion – chopped

1 clove garlic – crushed

225 g (8 oz) mushrooms – sliced

213 g (7.51 oz) tin red kidney beans – drained and rinsed

pepper

15 ml (1 tbsp) fresh oregano

397 g (14 oz) tin tomatoes

10 ml (1 dsp) cornflour

30 ml (2 tbsp) water

Cheese Sauce

50 g (2 oz) NI Butter

50 g (2 oz) plain flour

568 ml (1 pt) NI Milk

175 g (6 oz) NI Cheddar Cheese – grated

pepper

pinch nutmeg

225 g (8 oz) broccoli – cooked for 5 minutes

Bean Sauce – Melt butter and oil and sauté onion, garlic and mushrooms gently for 3–4 minutes. Add beans, pepper, oregano and tomatoes. Bring to the boil and simmer for 10 minutes. Mix cornflour with water, add to bean sauce, bring to boil and stir until thickened.

Sauce – Make by the all-in-one method. Remove from heat and stir in two-thirds of cheese, pep-per and nutmeg. Lightly oil las-agne dish. Make alternate layers of lasagne, bean sauce, broccoli and cheese sauce finishing with lasagne and cheese sauce. Sprinkle with remaining cheese and bake at 350°F, 180°C, Mark 4 for 30 minutes until golden brown.

Leek and Sweetcorn Potatoes

450 g (1 lb) potatoes

300 g (12 oz) tin sweetcorn – drained

1 leek – sliced thinly

150 ml (5.3 oz) NI Soured Cream

a little NI Milk

75 g (3 oz) fresh breadcrumbs – white or brown

pepper

Wash and parboil potatoes for 10 minutes. Drain, peel and slice thinly. Layer potatoes with corn and leeks in an oiled ovenproof dish. Mix together soured cream and milk. Season well, pour over potatoes. Bake at 375°F, 190°C, Mark 5 for one hour or until potatoes are cooked. After one hour sprinkle over bread-crumbs and return to the oven for a further 15 minutes.

Broccoli and Leek Casserole

450 g (1 lb) broccoli florets

450 g (1 lb) leeks – trimmed and sliced

Sauce

1 onion – chopped

2.5 ml (½ tsp) celery salt

25 g (1 oz) NI Butter

15 ml (1 tbsp) oil

25 g (1 oz) mixed nuts – chopped

50 g (2 oz) wholemeal flour

284 ml (½ pt) NI Milk

150 ml (¼ pt) vegetable stock – reserved

1.25 ml (¼ tsp) nutmeg – grated

black pepper

Topping

50 g (2 oz) brown breadcrumbs

25 g (1 oz) mixed nuts – chopped

25 g (1 oz) NI Butter – melted

Blanch vegetables for 5 minutes (reserve water for stock), and place in an oiled ovenproof dish. Keep warm.

Sauce – Fry onion and celery salt in butter and oil for 2 minutes, then add nuts and cook for 2 minutes. Add flour and cook for one minute. Gradually add milk and stock and stir until mixture cooks and thickens. Add nut-meg, season to taste. Pour sauce over vegetables and top with breadcrumbs and nuts, tossed in butter. Grill until crispy. Serve hot with pasta, garnished with paprika pepper.

near Claudy, Co. Londonderry

Pancakes,
Flans &
Pizzas

Pancakes, flans and pizzas have been grouped together for several reasons: they are simple to make once the basics of the flan case, the pizza base, or the pancake batter have been mastered. They are cheap to make and you are almost certain to have all the ingredients already in your food cupboard, if you are faced with some unexpected guests; and they are all extremely nutritious and delicious. Add to all that, the fact that they can be sweet or savoury, simple as Bacon and Onion Quiche, or as exotic as Flambéed Crêpés. It is easy to see why they should form part of any cook's repertoire.

Pancakes

Tossed Pancake Batter

100 g (4 oz) plain wholemeal or plain flour or a mixture of both
1 size 3 egg
284 ml (½ pt) NI Milk
knob of NI Butter – melted

Traditional Method – Place flour in a bowl, drop in egg and half of the milk and whisk together until smooth. Add remainder of milk and mix together. Fold in butter.

Food Processor – Place flour, egg and milk in food processor and blend until smooth. Add butter.

To Cook Pancakes – Pour enough batter onto a preheated, lightly oiled pan to coat the base thinly. Cook over a medium heat until browned. Flip over with palette knife or toss. Cook the second side. Turn onto a warmed plate. Repeat until batter is finished, interleaving pancakes with greaseproof paper. Keep warm if going to use immediately. Makes approximately 8 pancakes.

Variations to Batter –
1. Add chopped fresh herbs of choice.
2. Add 100 g (4 oz) frozen spinach – thawed and drained.

Chicken and Bean-Sprout Pancakes

8 tossed cooked pancakes
Filling
1 onion – chopped
25 g (1 oz) NI Butter – melted
100 g (4 oz) button mushrooms – sliced
75 g (3 oz) beansprouts
225 g (8 oz) cooked chicken – chopped
15 ml (1 tbsp) soy sauce
pepper
parsley – chopped

Cook onion in butter until soft. Add mushrooms, bean sprouts and chicken, cook for 2 minutes. Add sauce and pepper. Fill pancakes. Roll up and garnish with parsley.

Cheese and Raisin Pancakes (illustrated)

8 tossed cooked pancakes
Filling
227 g (8 oz) NI natural Cottage Cheese .
50 g (2 oz) raisins
25 g (1 oz) walnuts – chopped
5 ml (1 tsp) ground cinnamon
pinch ground nutmeg
25 g (1 oz) demerara sugar
½ orange – rind and juice
30 ml (2 tbsp) honey

Mix cheese, raisins, and walnuts together. In a separate bowl, mix cinnamon, nutmeg, sugar and orange rind. Stir half the spiced sugar mixture into the cheese mixture. Fill pancakes and roll up loosely. Place seam up in a lightly oiled ovenproof dish. Warm honey, mix with orange juice and pour over pancakes. Sprinkle with remaining spiced sugar mixture. Bake at 350°F, 180°C, Mark 4 for 12–15 minutes until golden and slightly crisp. Serve hot with natural yogurt.

Flambéed Crêpes

8 tossed cooked pancakes
Filling
100 g (4 oz) NI Butter
90 g (3½ oz) granulated sugar
½ lemon – rind
100 g (4 oz) flaked almonds
60 ml (4 tbsp) orange juice
45 ml (3 tbsp) lemon juice
15 ml (1 tbsp) Cherry Brandy
15 ml (1 tbsp) Cognac
425 g (15 oz) tin peach halves – drained
60 ml (4 tbsp) Calvados/Cointreau

Filling – Place butter, sugar, lemon rind and almonds in a saucepan, and heat for 5 minutes without stirring, until sugar caramelises. Stir in lemon and orange juices, Cherry Brandy and Cognac, cook for a few minutes. Add fruit and folded crêpes and cook for 3 minutes frequently spooning syrup over. To flambé – warm Calvados/Cointreau in a ladle, pour over crêpes and set alight.

Yogurt Pancakes

2 size 3 eggs
2 x 125 g (4.4 oz) NI natural Yogurt
50 g (2 oz) plain wholemeal flour
50 g (2 oz) plain flour
2.5 ml (½ tsp) baking powder – sieved
15 g (½ oz) NI Butter – melted

Make up as tossed pancake batter.

Scotch Pancakes

100 g (4 oz) soda-bread flour
25 g (1 oz) caster sugar – optional
1 size 3 egg
190 ml (⅓ pt) NI Buttermilk

Sieve flour into mixing bowl and add sugar. Make a well in the centre and using a wooden spoon gradually blend in the egg and buttermilk. Beat well. Heat pan, coat lightly with oil. Drop individual tablespoons of mixture into the pan. Cook for one minute. Flip pancakes over to cook the second side.

Toppings

1. Fresh lemon juice and caster sugar.
2. Spread with NI Butter.
3. Fresh NI Whipped Dairy Cream and raspberry jam.
4. Sieved NI Cottage Cheese and chopped fresh fruit mixed together.

Flans

Shortcrust Pastry – Made by the traditional "rubbing-in" method or by the "food processor" method. The latter has the advantage of speed and also the ingredients are kept cool, an important factor in pastry making.

Shortcrust Pastry

175 g (6 oz) plain flour
75 g (3 oz) NI Butter
30 ml (6 tsp) NI Milk
with food processor use 45 ml (3 tbsp) NI Milk

Rich Shortcrust Pastry

175 g (6 oz) plain flour
75 g (3 oz) NI Butter
1 size 3 egg – beaten

Sweet Shortcrust Pastry

175 g (6 oz) plain flour
75 g (3 oz) NI Butter
25 g (1 oz) caster sugar
30 ml (6 tsp) NI Milk
with food processor use 45 ml (3 tbsp) NI Milk

Wholemeal Pastry

75 g (3 oz) plain wholemeal flour
40 g (1½ oz) plain flour
40 g (1½ oz) self-raising flour
75 g (3 oz) NI Butter
30 ml (6 tsp) NI Milk
with food processor use 45 ml (3 tbsp) NI Milk

Rubbing in Method
1. Place dry ingredients in a bowl and rub in the butter, until the mixture resembles fine breadcrumbs.

2. Mix to a firm dough with milk or egg.

3. Refrigerate for ½ hour (this prevents shrinkage).

4. Pastry is then ready to roll out.

Food Processor Method
Place the dry ingredients in the bowl with the butter cut into 2.5 cm (1 in.) pieces. Process until the mixture resembles fine breadcrumbs (10–15 seconds). Add the liquid through the feed tube while the motor is running and process until the mixture forms a ball around the blade.

For all recipes use a 20 cm (8 in) flan ring.

To Line a Flan Ring

Flans are baked in plain or fluted rings set on baking trays or in a French fluted flan tin with a loose base or in a ceramic dish. It is best to use metal rather than porcelain or glass dishes for flans because it is a much better conductor of heat, so will give a crisp, evenly cooked pastry. A pre-baked flan case with a filling cooked in it will give better results than a filling in an uncooked flan case and cooking both together.

1. Roll out pastry as thinly as possible into a circle 5 cm (2 in.) wider than the ring.

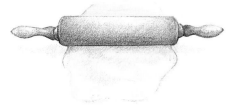

2. Lift the pastry onto the ring with the rolling pin.

3. Line the ring carefully making sure there is no air trapped between the pastry and the ring. If using a *plain* ring, trim pastry just above the rim and knock up the edges; if a *fluted* ring is used, press pastry against inner fluted ring edges, then cut pastry level with rim.

4. *Bake blind* – Line pastry case with greaseproof paper and weigh it down with dried or aluminium baking beans. Bake at 350°F, 180°C, Mark 4 for 15–20 minutes.

5. Remove from oven and place on cooling tray. Allow to cool thoroughly before removing ring.

6. Use immediately, or store in a cake tin or freeze in a sealed container.

Bacon & Onion Quiche (not illustrated)

Pastry
15 ml (1 tbsp) NI Milk
114 g (4 oz) NI natural Cottage Cheese – sieved
50 g (2 oz) NI Butter – melted
100 g (4 oz) plain flour

Filling
15 g (½ oz) NI Butter
1 onion – chopped
100 g (4 oz) bacon – chopped
114 g (4 oz) NI Cottage Cheese with chives
2 size 3 eggs
142 ml (¼ pt) NI Milk
pepper

Pastry – Mix milk, cottage cheese and butter together. Sieve flour, combine with cheese mixture to form a soft dough. Refrigerate for half an hour. Roll out to line 20 cm (8 in.) flan ring.

Filling – Melt butter, sauté onion and bacon then fold in cheese. Whisk eggs and milk together, season and fold in onion and bacon mixture. Pour into flan case and bake at 400°F, 200°C, Mark 6 for 20–25 minutes. Garnish with snipped chives.

NB Alternatively use wholemeal shortcrust pastry flan case.

The above pastry can be difficult to work with.

Courgette Wheat Flan

Wholemeal Shortcrust Pastry

100 g (4 oz) NI Butter
100 g (4 oz) plain wholemeal flour
50 g (2 oz) plain flour
50 g (2 oz) self-raising flour
60–75 ml (4–5 tbsp) NI Milk

Filling

225 g (8 oz) courgettes – sliced
25 g (1 oz) NI Butter
5 ml (1 tsp) cooking oil
1 onion – chopped
198 g (7 oz) tin tuna fish – drained
125 ml (4.4 fl oz) fresh NI Whipping Cream
3 size 3 eggs
142 ml (¼ pt) NI Milk
100 g (4 oz) NI Cheddar Cheese – grated
pepper

Pastry – Make pastry and use to line 22 cm (9 in.) flan ring. Refrigerate for 30 minutes and bake blind at 350°F, 180°C, Mark 4 for 15 minutes.

Filling – Fry courgettes in butter and oil. Add onion and cook until golden brown. Meanwhile spread tuna fish over pastry case and spoon courgettes and onion on top. Beat together cream, eggs, milk, cheese and seasoning. Pour into flan case and bake at 375°F, 190°C, Mark 5 for 25–30 minutes. Serve hot.

Cheese and Mackerel Soufflé Flan

Shortcrust Pastry

225 g (8 oz) plain flour
100 g (4 oz) NI Butter
60–75 ml (4–5 tbsp) NI Milk

Filling

225 g (8 oz) smoked mackerel – cooked and flaked

Sauce

15 g (½ oz) NI Butter
15 g (½ oz) plain flour
142 ml (¼ pt) NI Milk
50 g (2 oz) NI Wensleydale Cheese – grated
pepper
pinch of mustard
2 size 3 eggs – separated
1 size 3 egg white

Pastry – Make pastry and use to line a 22 cm (9 in.) flan ring. Refrigerate for 30 minutes. Bake blind at 350°F, 180°C, Mark 4 for 15 minutes. Spread with fish.

Sauce – Make sauce by the all-in-one method. Add cheese, pepper and mustard. Add beaten egg yolks and cool. Whisk egg whites until they just stand in peaks. Fold into sauce. Pour into flan ring. Bake at 425°F, 220°C, Mark 7 for 25 minutes until risen, golden brown and set.

Bacon and Leek Flan

Wholemeal Shortcrust Pastry

100 g (4 oz) NI Butter
100 g (4 oz) plain wholemeal flour
100 g (4 oz) plain flour
60–75 ml (4–5 tbsp) NI Milk

Filling

25 g (1 oz) NI Butter
15 ml (1 tbsp) oil
450 g (1 lb) leeks – cut in thin slices
100 g (4 oz) back bacon – chopped
2.5 ml (½ tsp) nutmeg
100 g (4 oz) NI Cheddar Cheese – grated
2 size 3 eggs – beaten
125 ml (4.4 fl oz) fresh NI Whipping Cream
142 ml (¼ pt) NI Milk
pepper

Pastry – Make pastry and use to line a 22 cm (9 in.) flan ring. Refrigerate for 30 minutes and bake blind at 350°F, 180°C, Mark 4 for 15 minutes.

Filling – Heat the butter and oil in a saucepan, add the leeks, bacon and nutmeg. Cover and cook gently for about 10 minutes; cool. Whisk cheese, eggs, cream and milk together. Season. Pile leek mixture into pastry case then pour over the custard mixture. Bake at 350°F, 180°C, Mark 4 for 30–35 minutes.

Apple Poppy Seed Flan

Pastry

75 g (3 oz) plain wholemeal flour
40 g (1½ oz) plain flour
40 g (1½ oz) self-raising flour
75 g (3 oz) NI Butter
50 g (2 oz) caster sugar
1 size 3 egg – beaten

Filling

450 g (1 lb) dessert apples – peeled, cored and sliced
1 size 3 egg – beaten
142 ml (¼ pt) NI Milk
50 g (2 oz) caster sugar
25 g (1 oz) NI Butter – melted
1 lemon – rind
15 ml (1 tbsp) blue poppy seeds

Pastry – Make pastry using the egg as the binding ingredient and use to line 18 cm (7 in.) flan ring. Refrigerate for 30 minutes. Bake blind at 350°F, 180°C, Mark 4 for 15 minutes.

Filling – Place apple slices in flan ring. Mix egg, milk, sugar, butter and lemon rind together and pour over apples. Sprinkle with poppy seeds. Bake at 375°F, 190°C, Mark 5 for 30–40 minutes or until set.

Orange Rhubarb Flan

Pastry

100 g (4 oz) plain wholemeal flour
50 g (2 oz) plain flour
50 g (2 oz) self-raising flour
100 g (4 oz) NI Butter
50 g (2 oz) caster sugar
1 size 3 egg – beaten
a little milk if necessary

Filling

550 g (1¼ lb) rhubarb – trimmed and cut into 1.25 cm (½ in.) lengths
sugar to taste (optional)
40 g (1½ oz) raisins
2 size 3 eggs
50 g (2 oz) caster sugar
25 g (1 oz) plain flour – sieved
200 ml (7 fl oz) NI Milk
1 orange – rind and juice
1 orange – peeled and sliced
60 ml (4 tbsp) marmalade

Pastry – Make pastry using egg and milk as the binding ingredients and use to line 28 cm (11 in.) flan ring. Refrigerate for 30 minutes. Bake blind at 350°F, 180°C, Mark 4 for 15 minutes. Cool.

Filling – Spread rhubarb on base of flan and sprinkle with sugar if desired. Sprinkle with raisins. Whisk eggs, sugar and flour together and gradually whisk in milk. Heat gently then pour on top of the rhubarb. Scatter orange rind over. Arrange orange slices over the flan. Bake at 350°F, 180°C, Mark 4 for 45–50 minutes. Heat the marmalade with juice of the orange to make a glaze. Brush over the flan. Serve hot or cold.

Banana Hazelnut Tart

Base

50 g (2 oz) roasted hazelnuts – ground
50 g (2 oz) plain wholemeal flour
40 g (1½ oz) NI Butter
25 g (1 oz) soft brown sugar

Filling

50 g (2 oz) soft brown sugar
50 g (2 oz) NI Butter
1 orange – rind and juice
45 ml (3 tbsp) rum/brandy
1 kg (2 lb) ripe bananas – sliced
250 ml (8.8 fl oz) fresh NI Whipping Cream – whipped
2 x 125 g (4.4 oz) NI mandarin Yogurt

Base – Fold hazelnuts into flour. Rub in butter and mix in sugar. Press into base of oiled 20 cm (8 in.) loose-bottomed cake tin and bake at 375°F, 190°C, Mark 5 for 25–30 minutes. Leave to cool.

Filling – Melt butter with sugar, stir in orange juice and rum/brandy. Bring to boil, add banana slices and simmer for 3–5 minutes. Cool. Drain bananas and pile on top of base. (Reserve liquid.) Fold cream into yogurt and orange rind. Spoon on top of bananas. Chill thoroughly before serving. Serve reserved liquid separately.

Pizzas

Yeast Dough Base

225 g (8 oz) plain flour – sieved
5 ml (1 tsp) salt
1.25 ml (¼ tsp) sugar
7.5 ml (1½ tsp) Easy Blend dried yeast
1 size 3 egg – beaten
75–100 ml (3–4 fl oz) NI Milk – heated
5 ml (1 tsp) oil

Base – Place flour and salt in a bowl. Make a well in the centre and stir in sugar, yeast and egg. Gradually pour in enough milk to draw mixture together until it is a soft pliable dough. Transfer to a floured working surface and knead for about 10 minutes until smooth and fairly elastic. Replace the dough into bowl and rub the surface all over with oil. Then place a clean, damp cloth over the bowl and leave in a warmish place to rise for about one hour or until it has doubled in size. When the dough has "proved" (ie doubled in size), knead it again for about 5 minutes. Then roll it out into a circle approx 20 cm (8 in) in diameter and place on an oiled pizza plate or baking sheet.

58

Wholemeal Scone Base

100 g (4 oz) self-raising wholemeal flour – sieved
50 g (2 oz) self-raising flour – sieved
pepper
10 ml (1 dsp) fresh basil
10 ml (1 dsp) fresh oregano
25 g (1 oz) NI Butter
NI Milk

Place dry ingredients in a bowl and rub in the butter. Mix to an elastic dough with milk. Turn onto a floured board and knead lightly. Roll out into a circle approximately 20 cm (8 in.) in diameter and place on an oiled pizza plate or baking sheet.

Tuna Fish Topping

198 g (7 oz) tin tuna fish – drained
5 ripe tomatoes – sliced
1 green pepper – sliced into rings
10 black olives – stoned
pepper
paprika pepper
5 ml (1 tsp) fresh marjoram
5 ml (1 tsp) fresh basil
5 ml (1 tsp) fresh lemon balm
75 g (3 oz) NI Cheddar Cheese – grated

Layer fish, tomatoes, pepper, olives, seasoning and herbs on to base. Top with cheese and bake at 425°F, 220°C, Mark 7 for 20–25 minutes.

Tomato and Mushroom Topping

Tomato Sauce

1 large onion – chopped
2 cloves garlic – crushed
25 g (1 oz) NI Butter
397 g (14 oz) tin tomatoes – drained and chopped
30 ml (2 tbsp) tomato purée
2.5 ml (½ tsp) fresh basil
2.5 ml (½ tsp) fresh oregano

Topping

100 g (4 oz) button mushrooms – sliced
50 g (2 oz) ham – sliced into strips
1 green pepper – deseeded and sliced
50 g (2 oz) tinned pineapple – chopped (optional)
75 g (3 oz) NI Cheddar Cheese
pepper

Sauce – Cook onion and garlic in butter until soft. Add remaining ingredients. Simmer for 10–15 minutes until thick. Cool. Spread sauce over pizza base.

Topping – Arrange mushrooms, ham, pepper and pineapple on top of sauce. Sprinkle cheese over, and season. Bake at 425°F, 220°C, Mark 7 for 30 minutes.

Ballygawley, Co. Tyrone

Soufflés, Mousses & Roulades

Savoury or sweet, starter or snack, first course through to last, these dishes have a lot to offer even the most inexperienced cook.

A souffle can seem to take on a life of its own as it rises . . . and rises. Mousses can sometimes seem slow to set, and roulades reluctant to roll. But these recipes are not at all difficult.

So do not be put off. For a party piece or a family treat, mould a mousse, roll a roulade, or stir up a souffle!

Preparation of Soufflé Dish – for a cold soufflé

1. Fold a piece of greaseproof paper in half lengthwise making sure it is long enough to encircle the dish and that it extends the rim by 5 cm (2 in.).
2. Wrap the band around the dish. Keep the folded edge at the base and the cut edge uppermost for a better circular shape.
3. Tie securely with a piece of string or an elastic band.
4. Spoon the mixture into the dish until it reaches about 2.5 cm (1 in.) above the rim of the dish.
5. When soufflé has set, remove the string and remove paper band by holding blade of palette knife in boiling water for a few seconds and running between double thickness of greaseproof paper. Remove paper band.

Lemon Soufflé with Puréed Apricots

50 ml (2 fl oz) NI Milk
4 size 3 eggs – separated
100 g (4 oz) caster sugar
2 lemons – rind and juice
2 drops vanilla essence
2 x 15 g (½ oz) gelatine
3 x 125 g (4.4 oz) NI natural Yogurt
125 ml (4.4 fl oz) fresh NI Whipping Cream – whipped
411 g (14½ oz) tin apricot halves in natural juice – liquidised

Heat the milk in a bowl over a saucepan of warm water then whisk in the egg yolks, sugar, lemon rind and vanilla and stir until cooked. Cool. Dissolve gelatine in lemon juice in a bowl over a saucepan of hot water and add to creamed mixture. Place in refrigerator until just beginning to set. Then fold in yogurt and cream. Whisk egg whites until stiff and fold into mixture. Pour into a prepared 825 ml (1½ pt) soufflé dish or individual glass dishes. Chill to set. Decorate with a little more whipped cream and grated lemon rind. Serve with puréed apricots.

Haddock and Cucumber Soufflé

(not illustrated)

450 g (1 lb) smoked haddock fillets – skinned
426 ml (¾ pt) NI Milk
50 g (2 oz) NI Butter
65 g (2½ oz) plain flour
black pepper
114 g (4 oz) NI natural Cottage Cheese
½ small cucumber – diced
2 size 3 eggs – separated
30 ml (2 tbsp) spring onions – chopped

Simmer the fish in the milk for 8 minutes. Drain, reserving the liquid. Flake the fish and remove the bones. Make sauce with the butter, flour and reserved milk using the all-in-one method. Season. Fold in the cottage cheese, fish, cucumber, egg yolks and spring onions. Whisk the egg whites until stiff and fold into the soufflé mixture. Pour into an oiled 1.7 litre (3 pt) soufflé dish and bake at 400°F, 200°C, Mark 6 for 35 minutes or until well risen and golden.

Mango Soufflé

1 large or 2 small ripe mangoes – peeled and stoned
50 g (2 oz) caster sugar
1 lemon – juice
30 ml (2 tbsp) water
15 g (½ oz) gelatine
125 ml (4.4 fl oz) fresh NI Whipping Cream – whipped
2 size 3 egg whites

Purée mango flesh with sugar. Dissolve gelatine in lemon juice and water in a bowl over a saucepan of hot water. Cool and add to mango purée. Leave in fridge until just beginning to set. Fold in cream and whisked egg whites. Pour into a prepared 825 ml (1½ pt) soufflé dish or individual glass dishes. Chill until set. Serve with whipped dairy cream.

Caramel Soufflé

Caramel

100 g (4 oz) granulated sugar
60 ml (4 tbsp) water
85 ml (3 fl oz) warm water

Soufflé

3 size 3 eggs
2 egg yolks
100 g (4 oz) caster sugar
15 g (½ oz) gelatine
45 ml (3 tbsp) water
250 ml (8.8 fl oz) fresh NI Double Cream – whipped
50 g (2 oz) peanut brittle – crushed

Caramel – Place sugar and water in a saucepan. Heat gently until the sugar dissolves, then bring to the boil and cook to a rich chestnut coloured caramel. Remove from the heat and carefully add warm water. Heat gently until the caramel dissolves, then leave to cool.

Soufflé – Whisk eggs, yolks and sugar together in a bowl over a saucepan of warm water until the mixture is very thick and light. Dissolve gelatine in water in a bowl over a saucepan of hot water. Stir gently into egg mixture; leave until just beginning to set. Fold in cream and cooled caramel. When thoroughly blended pour into a prepared 825 ml (1½ pt) soufflé dish or individual glass dishes. Chill until set. Decorate with whipped cream and sprinkle with peanut brittle. Serve with fresh fruit salad.

Cider Cheese Soufflé

150 ml (¼ pt) dry cider

85 ml (3 fl oz) NI Milk

1 onion – quartered

1 carrot – quartered

1 stick celery – quartered

1 bay leaf

6 peppercorns

25 g (1 oz) NI Butter

25 g (1 oz) plain flour

5 ml (1 tsp) French mustard

cayenne pepper and grated nutmeg

100 g (4 oz) NI Cheddar Cheese – grated

4 size 3 eggs – separated

Oil a 1.1 litre (2 pt) soufflé dish. Put the cider, milk, onion, carrot, celery, bay leaf and peppercorns in a saucepan and bring to almost boiling point, remove from heat, cover and leave to infuse for 15 minutes. Strain. Reserve liquid. Make a sauce with the butter, flour and reserved liquid by the all-in-one method. Add the mustard, pepper, nutmeg and cheese and mix well. Cool the sauce for a few minutes and beat in the egg yolks. Whisk the egg whites stiffly and carefully fold in. Pour into soufflé dish and bake at 350°F, 180°C, Mark 4 for 30–35 minutes or until puffed and golden. Serve immediately.

Salmon and Prawn Mousse

450 g (1 lb) salmon – poached and flaked	
100 g (4 oz) prawns	
2 size 3 eggs – hard-boiled and chopped	
whole prawns – to decorate	

Béchamel Sauce

284 ml (½ pt) NI Milk	
bouquet garni	
6 peppercorns	
20 g (¾ oz) NI Butter	
20 g (¾ oz) plain flour	

45 ml (3 tbsp) water	
15 g (½ oz) gelatine	
60 ml (4 tbsp) mayonnaise	
pepper, tabasco sauce, lemon juice	
15 ml (1 tbsp) tomato ketchup	
125 ml (4.4 fl oz) fresh NI Double Cream – whipped	

Mix the salmon, prawns and eggs together.

Sauce – Heat milk with the bouquet garni and peppercorns until it just reaches boiling point. Remove from heat, and leave for 5 minutes. Strain. Reserve milk. Make a sauce with butter, flour and reserved milk by the all-in-one method. Leave until cold. Dissolve gelatine in water in a bowl over a saucepan of hot water, then stir into sauce. Add mayonnaise, pepper, tabasco, lemon juice, tomato ketchup and fish mixture. Mix well. Fold cream into the mixture. Pour into individual ramekin dishes or into a 1.1 litre (2 pt) mould. Chill until set. Unmould and garnish with whole prawns or a sprig of dill.

Peach & Lemon Mousse

3 size 3 eggs

50 g (2 oz) caster sugar

1 lemon – rind and juice

3 ripe peaches/nectarines – skinned

15 g (½ oz) gelatine

284 ml (½ pt) NI Buttermilk

1 peach for decoration

Place eggs, sugar and finely grated lemon rind in a large bowl and whisk together over a saucepan of warm water until mixture is pale, thick and creamy. Chop the fruit, discard the stones and process with 15 ml (1 tbsp) lemon juice to make a smooth purée. Gradually whisk purée into mousse mixture. Dissolve gelatine in 45 ml (3 tbsp) lemon juice, in a bowl over a saucepan of hot water. Cool, then add to the mousse mixture with buttermilk. Stir thoroughly to mix. Pour into a glass bowl and chill to set. Decorate with slices of peach.

Raspberry Mousse

3 size 3 eggs – separated

50 g (2 oz) caster sugar

225 g (8 oz) raspberries – sieved

1 lemon – juice

15 g (½ oz) gelatine

125 g (4.4 oz) NI natural Yogurt

Place egg yolks and sugar in a bowl over a saucepan of hot water and whisk together until the mixture cooks and thickens. Cool. Stir in raspberries. Dissolve gelatine in lemon juice in a bowl over a saucepan of hot water. Add to creamed mixture. Cool. Fold in yogurt. Whisk egg whites until stiff and fold into mixture. Pour into a glass bowl or individual glass dishes. Chill to set. Decorate with whipped dairy cream.

Blackcurrant and Yogurt Mousse

450 g (1 lb) blackcurrants – stems removed

30 ml (2 tbsp) cassis or blackcurrant syrup

45 ml (3 tbsp) water

15 g (½ oz) gelatine

100g (4 oz) caster sugar

2 x 125 g (4.4 oz) NI natural Yogurt

2 size 3 eggs – whites

Stew blackcurrants with either cassis or syrup, until soft. Add half the sugar and stir until dissolved. Purée. Dissolve gelatine in water in a bowl over a saucepan of hot water and stir into the blackcurrant purée. Cool. Fold in yogurt. Whisk egg whites until stiff, and gradually whisk in the sugar. Fold into the blackcurrant mixture and turn into a glass bowl. Chill until set. Decorate with whipped dairy cream.

Roulades

Roulade means literally "a rolling" in French and is a term traditionally applied to a piece of meat rolled round a stuffing. However it can also be used for other rolled dishes. Today the term has broadened to mean a no-flour sponge roll (sweet or savoury) whisked to an airy lightness and gently rolled up swiss roll style. A roulade is a variation on the soufflé; both using the same basic ingredients. Serve the roulade with cocktails, as a starter, as a main course or a supper dish or for any occasion when you want something special for a good party piece!

Preparing a Swiss Roll Tin

Oil a swiss roll tin measuring 30 x 20 cm (12 in. x 8 in.) and line with greaseproof paper, cutting neatly into the corners. Oil greaseproof paper.

Nutty Orange Roulade

Roulade

4 size 3 eggs – separated
125 g (5 oz) caster sugar
25 g (1 oz) ground almonds
1.25 ml (¼ tsp) almond essence
25 g (1 oz) flaked almonds

Filling

250 ml (8.8 fl oz) fresh NI Double Cream – whipped
60 ml (4 tbsp) dry white wine
3 oranges – peeled, segmented, chopped and drained

Whisk egg yolks and sugar together until creamy and thick. Fold in ground almonds and essence. Whisk egg whites until stiff, fold into yolk mixture. Pour into prepared swiss roll tin, scatter flaked almonds over. Bake at 400°F, 200°C, Mark 6 for 15 minutes. Remove from oven, leaving roulade in the tin, cover with a clean tea towel and leave until cold. Fold wine and oranges into cream. Turn roulade onto greaseproof paper (dusted with caster sugar). Remove lining. Spread filling over roulade. Roll up and decorate with shreds of orange rind. Serve chilled.

Chocolate and Raspberry Roulade

Roulade

175 g (6 oz) plain dark chocolate – broken into pieces
45 ml (3 tbsp) hot water
5 size 3 eggs – separated
125 g (5 oz) caster sugar

Filling

62 g (2.2 oz) NI natural Yogurt
250 ml (8.8 fl oz) fresh NI Double Cream – whipped
225 g (8 oz) raspberries

Place chocolate and water in a bowl and melt over a saucepan of hot water. Cool. Whisk egg whites until stiff, fold gently into the chocolate mixture. Pour into prepared swiss roll tin. Bake at 350°F, 180°C, Mark 4 for 15–20 minutes. Remove from oven, leaving roulade in the tin, cover with a clean tea towel and leave until cold. Gently fold yogurt into cream. Turn roulade onto greaseproof paper sprinkled with icing sugar. Remove lining. Spread cream and yogurt mixture over roulade to within 5 cm (2 in.) on one short edge. Cover with raspberries and roll up.

Spinach Roulade

Roulade

450 g (1 lb) fresh spinach or 175 g
(6 oz) frozen spinach – defrosted

4 size 3 eggs – separated

½ tsp (2.5 ml) anchovy essence

½ small bulb fresh fennel – chopped

5 ml (1 tsp) fresh dill – chopped

black pepper

Filling

341 g (12 oz) NI natural Cottage
Cheese – sieved

½ small bulb fresh fennel – chopped

5 ml (1 tsp) fresh dill – chopped

175 g (6 oz) smoked salmon –
sliced into slivers

If using fresh spinach – remove stalks and wash well. Boil for 2–3 minutes. Drain well and liquidise. Beat egg yolks into the spinach, add essence, herbs and seasoning. Whisk egg whites until stiff and fold into spinach mixture. Pour into prepared swiss roll tin and bake at 375°F, 190°C, Mark 5 for 10–12 minutes or until the top feels spongy to touch. Turn roulade onto greaseproof paper, removing lining. Combine ingredients for filling reserving 25 g (1 oz) smoked salmon. Spread on to roulade and roll up. Garnish with reserved slivers of smoked salmon.

Pepperoni Roulade

(not illustrated)

Roulade

5 size 3 eggs – separated

1 red pepper – cored, deseeded,
finely chopped

10 ml (1 dsp) tomato purée

black pepper

Filling

1 onion – chopped

25 g (1 oz) NI Butter

1 courgette – chopped

213 g (7 oz) tin tomatoes

15 ml (1 tbsp) fresh marjoram –
chopped

black pepper

50 g (2 oz) NI Red Cheddar
Cheese – grated

62 g (2.2 oz) NI natural Yogurt

parsley

Fry onion in butter until soft. Add courgette, tomatoes, marjoram and pepper. Cook for 15 minutes, stirring occasionally until thick. Add cheese and yogurt. Keep hot. Whisk egg yolks, fold in pepper, tomato purée and pepper. Whisk egg whites until stiff and fold into egg yolk mixture. Pour into prepared swiss roll tin. Bake at 400°F, 200°C, Mark 6 for 15 minutes. Turn roulade onto greaseproof paper, removing lining. Spread hot filling over. Roll up and garnish with parsley.

Smoked Haddock Roulade

(not illustrated)

Roulade

225 g (8 oz) smoked haddock
fillets – skinned

284 ml (½ pt) NI Milk

4 size 3 eggs – separated

25 g (1 oz) NI Cheddar Cheese –
grated

pepper

Filling

25 g (1 oz) NI Butter

25 g (1 oz) plain flour

pinch ground nutmeg

2 hard-boiled eggs – chopped

parsley – chopped

Pour milk over haddock and simmer for 15 minutes. Remove haddock (reserve the milk), bone and flake it into a bowl. Add egg yolks, cheese and seasoning and mix together with 45 ml (3 tbsp) of the flavoured milk to soften the mixture. Whisk the egg whites until stiff and fold them into the fish mixture. Pour into a prepared swiss roll tin. Bake at 400°F, 200°C, Mark 6 for 10–12 minutes. Make up sauce by the all-in-one method using the 284 ml (½ pt) milk (reserved from the fish). Adjust seasoning and add nutmeg. Stir in eggs and parsley. Keep hot. Turn roulade onto greaseproof paper, removing lining. Spread hot filling over. Roll up and garnish with parsley.

Bûche de Noël

– the Traditional French Christmas Cake

Roulade

225 g (8 oz) plain chocolate – broken into pieces
5 ml (1 tsp) instant coffee powder
67 ml (4½ tbsp) water
5 size 3 eggs – separated
125 g (5 oz) caster sugar

Praline Cream Filling

25 g (1 oz) sugar
50 g (2 oz) whole blanched almonds
250 ml (8.8 fl oz) fresh NI Double Cream – whipped

Chocolate Cream Covering

250 ml (8.8 fl oz) fresh NI Double Cream
125 ml (4.4 fl oz) fresh NI Double Cream
75 g (3 oz) plain chocolate – melted

Chocolate Leaves

50 g (2 oz) plain chocolate – melted
6 small leaves – washed and dried

Roulade – Place chocolate, coffee and water in saucepan. Heat gently, stirring until smooth. Whisk egg yolks and sugar until creamy and thick. Stir in chocolate mixture. Whisk egg whites until stiff and fold gently into mixture. Pour into prepared swiss roll tin 30 x 20 cm (12 x 8 in.). Bake at 425°F, 220°C, Mark 7 for 12–14 minutes. Leave to cool overnight in tin. Cover with a clean tea-towel. The following day turn roulade on to well sug-ared greaseproof paper.

Remove lining paper. Spread praline filling over cake and roll up, place on serving plate. (The cake is very moist inside and inclined to break apart. The chocolate cream will cover cracks). Chill for 30 minutes before icing.

Praline – Line baking sheet with tin-foil and oil it. Melt sugar with almonds over a gentle heat. Cook until almonds are browned and sugar is caramel coloured. Pour on to baking sheet. Leave to harden – about 1 hour. Crush to a powder with a rolling pin. Fold praline powder into cream.

Chocolate Cream Covering – Whip cream until it just holds its shape. Fold in the chocolate. Spread to cover roulade and mark lines with a pointed knife.

Chocolate Leaves – Spoon a thick layer of chocolate on to under-side of each leaf. Leave to dry. Peel leaves carefully. Arrange on roulade and just before serving dust lightly with icing sugar. Chill for 30 minutes before serving.

near Newry, Co. Armagh

Desserts

Everyone needs to feel spoiled and pampered sometimes. What better way to make a fuss of the family than to round off a good meal with a delicious dessert? Whether it is fresh seasonal fruits with a good dollop of fresh dairy cream, a mouth-freshening sorbet, or an elegant crème caramel, the recipes in this section will be totally irresistible to all generations.

So go on: don't trifle with their feelings. Spoil them!

Apricot and Lemon Sorbet

(not illustrated)

411 g (14½ oz) tin apricots – liquidised

2 size 3 eggs – separated

50 g (2 oz) caster sugar

250 ml (8.8 fl oz) fresh NI Double Cream – whipped

1 lemon – rind and juice

15 ml (1 tbsp) apricot brandy (optional)

Whisk together egg yolks and sugar until pale and fluffy. Fold in the apricot purée. Fold rind and juice of lemon and apricot brandy into cream and fold into apricot mixture. Fold in the whisked egg whites. Pour the mousse into a dish suitable for the freezer. Freeze until firm. Remove from freezer 30 minutes before serving. Serve with thin biscuits.

Iced Raspberry Crush with Hot Blackberry Sauce

Raspberry Crush

225 g (8 oz) fresh or frozen raspberries – liquidised and sieved

125 g (4.4 oz) NI natural Yogurt

150 ml (5.3 oz) NI Soured Cream

50 g (2 oz) caster sugar

Sauce

50 g (2 oz) caster sugar

225 g (8 oz) fresh or frozen blackberries

30 ml (2 tbsp) water

Crush – Place all the ingredients in a bowl, and whisk until smooth. Pour the mixture into a freezer container and quick freeze for 1–2 hours until half frozen. Turn into a bowl and whisk again. Pour into a container and freeze until firm for 5–6 hours. To serve – spoon into individual glasses.

Sauce – Place ingredients in a saucepan, bring to the boil, then reduce the heat and simmer for 10 minutes or until the fruit is soft, stirring occasionally. Liquidise. Then sieve. Pour into a jug, and serve hot, with the raspberry crush.

Tropical Fruit Ring

284 ml (½ pt) NI Milk

2 size 3 eggs – separated

65 g (2½ oz) caster sugar

1 lemon – rind and juice

15 g (½ oz) gelatine

15 ml (1 tbsp) water

2 x 125 g (4.4 oz) NI natural Yogurt

Decoration

2 kiwi fruit – peeled and sliced

50 g (2 oz) black grapes – deseeded

50 g (2 oz) green grapes – deseeded

Heat milk gently just to boiling point. Whisk together egg yolks, sugar and lemon rind. Gradually whisk in the milk. Return to the saucepan and stir over a gentle heat until the custard is cooked. Cool. Dissolve gelatine in the lemon juice and water in a bowl over a saucepan of hot water and add to the custard mixture. Cool until mixture starts to thicken. Fold yogurt into the custard. Fold in the whisked egg whites. Pour into a lightly oiled 1.1 litre (2 pt) ring mould and chill until set. Unmould onto serving plate. Decorate the sides of the ring with kiwi slices and grapes. Fill centre with remaining grapes and kiwi fruit.

Custard

Blending Method

Blend custard powder or corn-flour with sugar (if used) and a little of the measured milk. Heat remainder of milk and add to blended custard powder or cornflour. Return to saucepan and cook, stirring continuously until custard thickens.

Crème Caramel

Caramel

100 g (4 oz) granulated sugar
45 ml (3 tbsp) cold water
30 ml (2 tbsp) hot water

Custard

4 size 3 eggs
50 g (2 oz) caster sugar
few drops vanilla essence
568 ml (1 pt) NI Milk

Caramel – Dissolve sugar in water, bring to the boil and boil rapidly until deep golden in colour. Add hot water and stir well. Pour into a well buttered 1.1 litre (2 pt) mould and tilt quickly to cover base.

Custard – Beat together eggs, sugar and essence. Heat milk – do not boil – and whisk gently into egg mixture and strain into mould. Bake in a bain-marie at 325°F, 170°C, Mark 3 for approximately one hour or until set. When completely cold, turn onto serving dish and serve with fresh dairy cream.

Citron Crunch

Custard

40 ml (4 dsp) custard powder
568 ml (1 pt) NI Milk
25 g (1 oz) caster sugar
50 g (2 oz) NI natural Cottage Cheese
125 ml (4.4 fl oz) fresh NI Whipping Cream
125 g (4.4 oz) NI natural Yogurt
1 lemon – rind and juice

Crunch

50 g (2 oz) NI Butter
50 g (2 oz) wholewheat breadcrumbs
50 g (2 oz) wholewheat digestive biscuits – crushed
25 g (1 oz) demerara sugar
25 g (1 oz) nuts – chopped

Custard – Make by the blending method and leave to cool. Frost 4 sundae dishes.

Crunch – Melt butter and add breadcrumbs and biscuits and toss together. Remove from heat and add the sugar and nuts. Place a small amount in the bottom of each dish, press well and leave in the refrigerator to firm a little. Reserve remainder.

Place cheese, cream, yogurt, rind and juice of lemon and custard into a blender and process for a few seconds. Spoon into sundae dishes and sprinkle remaining crunch mixture on top. Chill and decorate with strips of lemon rind.

NB To frost sundae dishes – brush edge of dishes with lightly whisked egg white, then dip into coloured caster sugar.

Blackberry and Chocolate Trifle

225 g (8 oz) chocolate swiss roll – sliced
450 g (1 lb) fresh or frozen blackberries
50 g (2 oz) cornflour
852 ml (1½ pt) NI Milk
100 g (4 oz) dark chocolate – broken
2 size 3 eggs – separated
100 g (4 oz) caster sugar
few drops vanilla essence
5 ml (1 tsp) vinegar

Arrange swiss roll in base of large pyrex ovenproof dish. Top with blackberries. Make custard by the blending method. Add chocolate and allow to melt through. Cool slightly, beat in egg yolks. Pour over blackberries.

Meringue – Whisk egg whites until stiff. Whisk in half of sugar until smooth and glossy. Fold in remainder, plus essence and vinegar. Spoon swirls of meringue over the custard. Bake at 350°F, 180°C, Mark 4 for 10–15 minutes. Serve hot or cold.

Raspberry Cremets

397 g (14 oz) tin raspberries in natural juice – drained
15 g (½ oz) gelatine
45 ml (3 tbsp) custard powder
426 ml (¾ pt) NI Milk
1 orange – rind
2 x 125 g (4.4 oz) NI natural Yogurt
15 ml (1 tbsp) sugar

Dissolve gelatine in 45 ml (3 tbsp) raspberry juice or water in a bowl over a saucepan of hot water. Blend custard powder with a little of the measured milk. Infuse orange rind in remaining milk over a gentle heat for about 5 minutes. Strain. Make custard by the blending method. Remove from the heat, stir in gelatine and pour into a bowl. Cover and allow to get cold but not set. Then add yogurt and sugar and whisk again. Fold in raspberries. Pour into serving bowl. Cover. Chill. **NB** Use fresh fruits in season – raspberries, redcurrants, blackcurrants, loganberries or blackberries.

Mini Raspberry Mousses

1 pk raspberry jelly
450 ml (¾ pt) boiling water
275 g (10 oz) fresh or frozen raspberries
22 ml (1½ tbsp) custard powder
15 ml (1 tbsp) caster sugar
284 ml (½ pt) NI Milk
125 g (4.4 oz) NI natural Yogurt.

Dissolve ½ jelly in 300 ml (½ pt) boiling water. Cool. Divide 50 g (2 oz) raspberries between 6 individual mousse moulds. Pour jelly over, chill until set. Make custard by the blending method and leave to cool. Dissolve remaining jelly in 150 ml (¼ pt) boiling water. Cool until just runny. Puree remaining raspberries with yogurt, custard and jelly. Pour over the set jellies. Chill overnight. Turn out and decorate with whipped dairy cream.

Alternatives:
1. Lime jelly with gooseberries (lightly cooked and sweetened).
2. Black cherry jelly with black cherries (stoned).

Raspberry Pudding with Lemon Sauce

225 g (8 oz) raspberries
25 g (1 oz) NI Butter
100 g (4 oz) caster sugar
1 lemon – rind and juice
142 ml (¼ pt) NI Milk
2 size 3 eggs – separated
25 g (1 oz) plain flour
125 ml (4.4 fl oz) fresh NI Whipping Cream

Spread raspberries over base of 570 ml (1 pt) soufflé dish. Cream butter and half of sugar with lemon rind. Beat in lemon juice. Whisk milk into egg yolks and add to the creamed mixture alternating with flour and remaining sugar, until well blended. Alternatively liquidise until smooth. Whisk egg whites until stiff and fold into mixture. Pour over raspberries and place dish in a roasting tin with 2.5 cm (1 in.) of water in the bottom. Cook for 40–45 minutes at 375°F, 190°C, Mark 5 until golden and set. Serve hot with pouring fresh dairy cream, or cold, decorated with whipped cream.

Savarin

75 g (3 oz) NI Butter
175 g (6 oz) strong plain flour
5 ml (1 tsp) caster sugar
pinch salt
10 ml (1 dsp) Easy Blend dried yeast
3 size 4 eggs – beaten
75 ml (5 tbsp) NI Milk

Syrup

100 g (4 oz) granulated sugar
150 ml (¼ pt) water
5 ml (1 tsp) lemon juice
2.5 cm (1 in.) cinnamon stick
5 coriander seeds – crushed
60 ml (4 tbsp) dark rum

Glaze

30 ml (2 tbsp) apricot jam

Savarin – Rub butter into flour until mixture resembles fine breadcrumbs. Add sugar, salt and yeast and mix thoroughly. Stir milk into eggs and blend slowly into dry ingredients to ensure a smooth consistency. Beat vigorously for 3–4 minutes. Oil a 22 cm (9 in) ring mould. Pour batter into ring mould, cover with an oiled polythene bag and leave in a warm place until batter has doubled in size. Bake at 400°F, 200°C, Mark 6 for 15 minutes. Leave to cool for 10 minutes, remove from tin, wipe tin and return the savarin.

Syrup – Gently heat water and sugar until dissolved, add lemon juice, cinnamon and coriander. Bring to boil and simmer for 10 minutes. Cool, strain and stir in rum. Prick savarin with a skewer. Pour the syrup over and leave for 2 hours. Turn onto serving plate, brush with hot jam. Fill the centre with fresh fruit and decorate with whipped fresh dairy cream.

Hot Plum Trifle

450 g (1 lb) plums
150 ml (¼ pt) water
100 g (4 oz) sugar
100 g (4 oz) sponge cake – sliced

Custard

60 ml (4 tbsp) cornflour
30 ml (2 tbsp) caster sugar
2 size 3 egg yolks
568 ml (1 pt) NI Milk

Meringue

2 size 3 egg whites
100 g (4 oz) caster sugar

Place plums and water in a saucepan, cover and stew until pulpy. Stir in sugar (skim off stones). Place sponge cake in 1.1 litre (2 pt) ovenproof dish and cover with stewed plums.

Custard – Whisk cornflour, sugar, egg yolks and 45 ml (3 tbsp) milk together. Heat remaining milk and add to mixture, stirring continuously. Return to saucepan and stir over low heat until custard thickens. Pour over plums.

Meringue – Whisk egg whites until stiff. Whisk in half of sugar until smooth and glossy, fold in remainder. Spoon meringue over custard. Bake at 350°C, 180°C, Mark 4 for 10–15 minutes.

Strawberry Trifle

225 g (8 oz) strawberries – hulled
60 ml (4 tbsp) dry sherry
30 ml (2 tbsp) icing sugar – sieved

Custard

45 ml (3 tbsp) cornflour
60 ml (4 tbsp) caster sugar
284 ml (½ pt) NI Milk
250 ml (8.8 fl oz) fresh NI Whipping Cream
3 size 3 egg yolks
2 size 3 egg whites
5 ml (1 tsp) vanilla essence
25 g (1 oz) NI Butter
1 jam filled swiss roll – cut into 8 slices
25 g (1 oz) flaked almonds – toasted

Reserve a few strawberries for decoration. Slice remainder and place in bowl with sherry and icing sugar to marinate for one hour.

Custard – Mix cornflour, sugar and a little of measured milk to give a smooth paste. Heat remaining milk and whipping cream in a double saucepan; pour onto cornflour paste, stirring vigorously. Return custard to saucepan. Bring to the boil stirring constantly until sauce cooks and thickens. Add egg yolks to custard, and stir until cooked. Add essence and butter. Leave covered, until just warm. Line base of a large bowl with swiss roll slices. Pile strawberries and juice on top. Whisk egg whites until stiff. Fold gently into custard and pour over strawberries. Chill. Decorate with strawberries and almonds.

Rum Spiced Ice Cream

100 g (4 oz) raisins
50 g (2 oz) glacé cherries – quartered
1.25 ml (¼ tsp) ground ginger
1.25 ml (¼ tsp) cinnamon
60 ml (4 tbsp) dark rum
30 ml (2 tbsp) port
1 orange – rind and juice
500 ml (17.6 fl oz) fresh NI Whipping Cream
3 size 3 egg yolks
100 g (4 oz) caster sugar

Place fruit, spices, rum, port and orange rind and juice together in a saucepan, bring to the boil, remove from heat, place lid on, and leave to get cold. Heat half of the cream to simmering point. Cream the egg yolks and sugar until thick and pale. Gradually pour on the hot cream, stirring continuously. Strain into a saucepan. Cook the custard slowly over a gentle heat, stirring continuously, until the mixture thickens. Cool. Whip remaining cream and fold into the cold custard. Pour into a container, cover and freeze until half frozen. Whisk thoroughly and fold in fruit mixture. Pour into a 1.1 litre (2 pt) loaf tin and freeze until firm. Turn out onto a cold serving plate and slice.

Quick Blackcurrant Ice Cream

325 g (12 oz) blackcurrants – fresh or frozen
225 g (8 oz) icing sugar – sieved
½ lemon – juice
250 ml (8.8 fl oz) fresh NI Double Cream – whipped

Liquidise the fruit and then sieve to get a smooth purée. Add the icing sugar and lemon juice and mix well. Gently fold cream into blackcurrant purée. Pour into a freezer container, cover and freeze until half frozen. Whisk thoroughly, then freeze until firm.
NB Alternatively use redcurrants in place of blackcurrants.

Lemon Ice Cream

284 ml (½ pt) NI Milk
3 lemons – juice and rind
2 size 3 eggs
175 g (6 oz) caster sugar
250 ml (8.8 fl oz) fresh NI Whipping Cream – whipped

Bring the milk almost to the boil with the lemon rind, then leave to infuse off the heat for about 15 minutes. Cream the eggs and sugar until thick and pale. Stir in the lemon flavoured milk and lemon juice and strain this mixture through a sieve into saucepan. Cook the custard slowly over a gentle heat, stirring continuously, until the mixture thickens. Cool. Fold the cream into the cooled custard. Pour into a freezer container, cover and freeze until half frozen. Whisk thoroughly, then freeze until firm.
NB For all ice-creams, transfer to the refrigerator for 20 minutes before serving.

Pear and Cardamon Ice Cream

450 g (1 lb) dessert pears – peeled, cored and sliced

30 ml (2 tbsp) honey

1 lemon – juice

50 g (2 oz) NI Butter

12 cardamon pods – slit pods and crush seeds

1 size 3 egg – beaten

1 egg yolk

125 ml (4.4 fl oz) fresh NI Double Cream – whipped

Cook pears in a covered saucepan with the honey, lemon juice, butter and crushed cardamon seeds. Liquidise, return to saucepan, add the eggs, stirring constantly over a gentle heat until mixture thickens. Chill. Fold in cream and pour into a freezer container. Cover and freeze until half frozen. Whisk thoroughly, then freeze until firm.

Quick Raspberry Ice Cream

225 g (8 oz) raspberries – fresh or frozen

50 g (2 oz) sugar

30 ml (2 tbsp) honey

3 x 125 g (4.4 oz) NI natural Yogurt

Liquidise fruit, sugar and honey. Add the yogurt, mix well and pour into a freezer container. Cover and freeze until half frozen. Whisk thoroughly, then freeze until firm.

Apple Ice Cream

4 size 3 egg yolks

100 g (4 oz) caster sugar

250 ml (8.8 fl oz) fresh NI Whipping Cream

675 g (1½ lbs) cooking apples – peeled, cored and sliced

Whisk the egg yolks with half of the sugar until very pale. Heat the cream to just below boiling point. Remove from the heat and whisk into the yolk mixture. Cook slowly over a gentle heat stirring continuously until the custard thickens. Cool. Stew the apples. Add the remaining sugar and liquidise. Sieve. Cool. Fold the apple purée into the custard. Pour into a freezer container, cover and freeze until half frozen. Whisk thoroughly, then freeze until firm.

Apricot Ice Cream

- 1.1 kg (2½ lb) fresh apricots – stoned
- 175 g (6 oz) caster sugar
- 150 ml (¼ pt) water
- 284 ml (½ pt) NI Milk – warmed
- 3 size 3 egg yolks
- 125 ml (4.4 fl oz) fresh NI Double Cream – whipped
- 125 g (4.4 oz) NI natural Yogurt
- 50 g (2 oz) meringues – crushed

Place apricots in a saucepan with half the sugar and water. Bring slowly to the boil to dissolve the sugar, then simmer until apricots are tender. Leave to cool. Liquidise. Cream egg yolks and remaining sugar until pale then pour the milk over, stirring constantly. Pour into a saucepan and cook over a gentle heat until custard thickens. Cool. Fold cream, yogurt and apricot purée into the custard. Pour into a freezer container, cover and freeze until half frozen. Whisk thoroughly, fold in the meringues, then freeze until firm.

Trassie Road, The Mournes, Co. Down

Baking

Mothers have been learning from their daughters when it comes to experimenting with more exotic ingredients. But the reverse is happening, with a return to traditional baking recipes.

Young, thoroughly modern women, with an eye to health and fitness, are turning to their mothers, experienced in the art of wholesome bread and cake making, for a few tips on achieving the appetising results which have been staple country kitchen fare for generations.

Many of the recipes in this section use wholemeal flour – recognising the trend towards adding a healthy, high fibre dimension to our diet.

Wholemeal Bread

175 g (6 oz) plain wholemeal flour – sieved	
100 g (4 oz) plain flour – sieved	
knob of NI Butter	
5 ml (1 tsp) baking soda – sieved	
5 ml (1 tsp) brown sugar	
2.5 ml (½ tsp) salt	
284 ml (½ pt) NI Buttermilk	

Place flours in a bowl, and rub in butter with the fingertips. Fold in dry ingredients and bind together with buttermilk to give a very soft consistency. Spoon into an oiled 450 g (1 lb) loaf tin and bake at 400°F, 200°C, Mark 6 for 10 minutes, then reduce to 350°F, 180°C, Mark 4 for 50 minutes. Turn out and cool.

Banana Bread

75 g (3 oz) NI Butter	
75 g (3 oz) caster sugar	
1 size 2 egg	
100 g (4 oz) self-raising flour	
1 large or 2 medium bananas – mashed	
Icing	
50 g (2 oz) icing sugar – sieved	
few drops lemon juice	

Cream butter and sugar together until light and fluffy. Beat in egg, then fold in flour and lastly bananas. Spoon into 450 g (1 lb) prepared loaf tin and bake at 350°F, 180°C, Mark 4 for 30–40 minutes. Leave to cool in tin.

Icing – Place sugar in a bowl and mix to a dropping consistency with lemon juice. Spoon icing over cake.

Date and Walnut Loaf

225 g (8 oz) stoned dates – chopped	
5 ml (1 tsp) baking soda	
pinch of salt	
300 ml (½ pt) hot water	
275 g (10 oz) self-raising flour	
100 g (4 oz) NI Butter	
50 g (2 oz) shelled walnuts – chopped	
100 g (4 oz) dark soft brown sugar	
1 size 3 egg – beaten	
Topping	
75 ml (5 tbsp) soft brown sugar	
30 ml (2 tbsp) NI Butter	
30 ml (2 tbsp) fresh NI Whipping Cream	
chopped walnuts	

Place dates, baking soda and salt into a bowl and pour over hot water. Set aside until cool. Meanwhile, sieve flour into a mixing bowl and rub in butter until mixture resembles fine breadcrumbs. Stir in walnuts and sugar. Mix the dry ingredients into the cooled date mixture and beat in the egg. Pour into a prepared 900 g (2 lb) loaf tin and bake at 350°F, 180°C, Mark 4 for 1–1¼ hours or until a skewer inserted in the centre comes out clean. Turn onto a cooling tray and leave to cool.

Topping – Place all ingredients in a saucepan, bring to the boil and boil for 3 minutes. Pour over loaf and decorate with walnuts.

Fruit and Nut Gingerbread

150 g (5 oz) plain flour – sieved
5 ml (1 tsp) ground cinnamon
15 ml (1 tbsp) ground ginger
10 ml (1 dsp) baking powder
150 g (5 oz) medium oatmeal
100 g (4 oz) dark muscovado sugar
60 ml (4 tbsp) treacle
100 g (4 oz) NI Butter
2 size 3 eggs – beaten
225 ml (8 fl oz) NI Milk
100 g (4 oz) sultanas
50 g (2 oz) flaked almonds – chopped – reserve a few to scatter on top.

Mix together flour, spices, baking powder, oats and sugar in a bowl. Warm treacle and butter together. Make a well in centre of dry ingredients and pour in treacle and butter, and eggs, and beat for 2 minutes. Stir in milk, sultanas and nuts and spoon mixture into a 900 g (2 lb) prepared loaf tin. Scatter almonds over. Bake at 350°F, 180°C, Mark 4 for 1½ hours.

Gingerbread (not illustrated)

30 ml (2 tbsp) golden syrup
30 ml (2 tbsp) black treacle
100 g (4 oz) NI Butter
100 g (4 oz) dark soft brown sugar
5 ml (1 tsp) ground ginger
7.5 ml (1½ tsp) ground cinnamon
175 g (6 oz) plain flour – sieved
142 ml (¼ pt) NI Milk
5 ml (1 tsp) baking soda – sieved
1 size 3 egg – beaten

Gently heat syrup, treacle, butter and sugar until melted. Cool. Place dry ingredients in a bowl; make a hollow in centre and pour in melted mixture, milk and egg. Stir briskly and pour into a prepared 18 cm (7 in.) square cake tin. Bake at 325°F, 170°C, Mark 3 for 1–1¼ hours.

Blue Poppy Seed Cake

50 g (2 oz) blue poppy seeds
225 ml (8 fl oz) NI Milk
225 g (8 oz) NI Butter
225 g (8 oz) caster sugar
3 size 3 eggs – separated
225 g (8 oz) plain wholemeal flour – sieved
5 ml (1 tsp) baking powder

Bring the poppy seeds to the boil in the milk, then turn off the heat and leave to soak for 25 minutes in a saucepan with the lid on. Cream butter and sugar together until light and fluffy, add the egg yolks, one at a time, and beat them in thoroughly. Mix flour and baking powder together and fold into the creamed mixture. Stir in the soaked poppy seeds and milk. Whisk the egg whites until they hold their shape and fold in carefully. Spoon the mixture into a prepared 20 cm (8 in.) cake tin and bake at 350°F, 180°C, Mark 4, for 70 minutes or until the centre feels firm. Let the cake stand in the tin for 10 minutes, then turn it onto a cooling rack.

Spiced Wholemeal Cake

150 g (5 oz) NI Butter
150 g (5 oz) soft dark brown sugar
2 size 3 eggs – beaten
275 g (10 oz) raisins
115 ml (4 fl oz) NI Milk
100 g (4 oz) self-raising flour – sieved
100 g (4 oz) plain wholemeal flour – sieved
5 ml (1 tsp) mixed spice
demerara sugar

Cream butter and sugar together until light and fluffy. Beat in eggs, a little at a time, adding a little of the flour if necessary to prevent curdling. Stir in raisins and milk. Fold in the flour and spice until evenly mixed. Place mixture in a prepared 18 cm (7 in.) cake tin and smooth top. Sprinkle with demerara sugar. Bake at 325°F, 170°C, Mark 3 for 1½ hours until risen and firm to touch.

Gingered Apple Swiss Roll

Sponge

2 size 3 eggs
50 g (2 oz) caster sugar
50 g (2 oz) plain flour – sieved
10 ml (1 dsp) ground ginger
2.5 ml (½ tsp) ground mixed spice
25 g (1 oz) NI Butter – melted

Filling

450 g (1 lb) cooking apples – peeled, cored and sliced
25 g (1 oz) NI Butter
2.5 ml (½ tsp) ground cinnamon
45 ml (3 tbsp) water
50 g (2 oz) granulated sugar
15 g (½ oz) root ginger – finely chopped
125 ml (4.4 fl oz) NI fresh Whipping Cream – whipped

Sponge – Whisk the eggs and sugar until very pale and thick. Fold in dry ingredients and cooled butter. Pour into a prepared swiss roll tin and bake at 400°F, 200°C, Mark 6 for 8–10 minutes. Turn out onto a sheet of greaseproof paper sprinkled with caster sugar. Remove lining paper. Trim off edges, roll up and leave to cool.

Filling – Cook apples, butter, cinnamon and water. When soft, beat to a purée with sugar and ginger. Cool. Unroll the rolled sponge. Spread with apple mixture, then with cream. Roll up.

Fruit Cake *(not illustrated)*

225 g (8 oz) NI Butter – softened
225 g (8 oz) dark soft brown sugar
275 g (10 oz) plain flour – sieved
10 ml (1 dsp) ground mixed spice – sieved
4 size 3 eggs – beaten
225 g (8 oz) seedless raisins
225 g (8 oz) sultanas
100 g (4 oz) mixed peel – chopped
100 g (4 oz) walnuts – chopped
120 ml (8 tbsp) Guinness

Oil and line 18 cm (7 in.) round cake tin. Cream butter and sugar until light and fluffy. Add eggs, flour and spice to the creamed mixture alternately, beating well between each addition to prevent curdling. Stir in fruit and walnuts. Add half the Guinness and stir well to make a soft dropping mixture. Spoon into the tin and bake at 325°F, 170°C, Mark 3 for 1 hour. Reduce to 300°F, 150°C, Mark 2 and continue cooking for 1¼ hours. Cover with a double layer of greaseproof paper, if cake begins to brown. Leave in the tin until cold and turn out onto a cooling tray, base upwards. Prick the base with a skewer and spoon over the remaining Guinness. Leave to stand for 45 minutes. Wrap in greaseproof paper and store in an airtight tin.

Chocolate Mallow Fridge Cake

Sandwich Cake

165 g (5½ oz) self-raising flour – sieved

15 g (½ oz) cocoa powder – sieved

175 g (6 oz) caster sugar

175 g (6 oz) NI Butter – softened

3 size 3 eggs

Filling

175 g (6 oz) marshmallows

30 ml (2 tbsp) sherry

125 ml (4.4 fl oz) fresh NI Double Cream – whipped

Covering

250 ml (8.8 fl oz) fresh NI Double Cream – whipped

50 g (2 oz) plain chocolate – grated

Cake – Place all ingredients in food mixer and cream together until light and fluffy. Divide mixture between 2 x 18 cm (7 in.) prepared sandwich tins and bake at 350°F, 180°C, Mark 4 for 20 minutes. Turn out onto cooling tray and cool.

Filling – Melt marshmallows (reserving 6) and sherry in a bowl over a saucepan of hot water – allow to become cold. Fold cream into marshmallow mixture. Leave until beginning to set. Slice sponge cakes to form 4 layers. Sandwich layers of cake with the mallow mixture beginning and ending with cake. Cover cake with the whipped cream and decorate with grated chocolate and pink marshmallows, lightly sprinkled with cocoa powder.

Magic Dragon Fluff

(not illustrated)

Sponge Cake

2 size 2 eggs

50 g (2 oz) caster sugar

50 g (2 oz) plain flour – sieved

Filling

15 g (½ oz) gelatine

45 ml (3 tbsp) water

25 g (1 oz) caster sugar

30 ml (2 tbsp) white wine

2 size 3 egg whites

3 x 125 g (4.4 oz) NI Yogurt – 1 muesli, 1 tropical fruit, 1 peach melba

150g (5 oz) milk chocolate

chocolate leaves

Sponge – Whisk together eggs and sugar until thick and creamy. Fold in flour and place in a prepared 20 cm (8 in.) sponge flan tin. Bake at 350°F, 180°C, Mark 4 for 12–15 minutes. Turn out onto a cooling tray.

Filling – Dissolve gelatine in water in a bowl over a saucepan of warm water and add to sugar and wine. Mix well. Fold in yogurts and whisked egg whites. Melt chocolate and spread a thin layer on base of flan case. Cool. Pour yogurt mixture into flan case and allow to set. Decorate with remainder of chocolate made into chocolate leaves.

Muesli Muffins

125 g (4.4 oz) NI natural Yogurt

142 ml (¼ pt) NI Milk

75 g (3 oz) muesli

50 g (2 oz) sultanas

50 g (2 oz) mixed nuts – chopped

1 size 3 egg – beaten

50 g (2 oz) NI Butter – melted and cooled

150 g (5 oz) plain flour – sieved

50 g (2 oz) soft brown sugar

15 ml (1 tbsp) baking powder

pinch salt

Combine yogurt and milk in a bowl, mix in muesli. sultanas and nuts. Add egg and butter and blend well. Add all at once to dry ingredients, stir until just moistened. Fill well-oiled patty tins with spoonfuls of the mixture. Bake at 400°F, 200°C, Mark 6 for 30 minutes. Serve warm.

Wholewheat Swiss Roll

Swiss Roll

3 size 3 eggs

75 g (3 oz) caster sugar

40 g (1½ oz) self-raising
wholemeal flour – sieved

40 g (1½ oz) self-raising flour –
sieved

30 ml (2 tbsp) warm water

Filling

62 g (2.2 oz) NI natural Yogurt

63 ml (2.2 fl oz) fresh NI Double
Cream – stiffly whipped

75 g (3 oz) fresh fruit – chopped

Whisk together eggs and sugar until thick and creamy. Fold in flours and water and spoon into prepared swiss roll tin. Bake at 425°F, 220°C, Mark 7 for 12–15 minutes. Turn out onto a piece of greaseproof paper, sprinkled with a little brown sugar. Remove lining, trim edges and roll up. Leave to cool.

Filling – Gently fold yogurt into cream and gradually fold in fruit. Unroll swiss roll, spread over filling and reroll.

Cinnamon Sponge

100 g (4 oz) NI Butter
100 g (4 oz) soft brown sugar
45 ml (3 tbsp) honey
3 size 3 eggs
250 g (9 oz) self-raising flour – sieved
5 ml (1 tsp) cinnamon
142 ml (¼ pt) NI Buttermilk

Cream butter and sugar together until light and fluffy, gradually beat in honey and eggs. Fold in flour, cinnamon and buttermilk alternately. Pour into a prepared 20 cm (8 in.) cake tin and bake at 350°F, 180°C, Mark 4 for 60–70 minutes. Remove from tin and sprinkle with caster sugar and leave to cool.

Carrot Cake

225 g (8 oz) plain wholemeal flour – sieved
10 ml (1 dsp) baking powder
100 g (4 oz) muscovado sugar
50 g (2 oz) walnuts – chopped
100 g (4 oz) carrots – grated
2 ripe bananas – mashed
2 size 3 eggs
115 ml (4 fl oz) corn oil

Topping

75 g (3 oz) NI Butter
75 g (3 oz) low fat cream cheese
175 g (6 oz) icing sugar – sieved
few drops vanilla essence
chopped walnuts

Oil and line a 28 cm x 18 cm (11 in. x 7 in.) oblong baking tin. Place the dry ingredients in a bowl with the walnuts and mix together. Add carrots, bananas, eggs and corn oil and beat well for one minute to give a soft consistency. Turn the mixture into the prepared cake tin and spread level. Bake at 350°F, 180°C, Mark 4 for 40 minutes or until the cake is well risen, and firm to the touch. Turn out and allow to cool.

Topping – Cream butter, cheese, icing sugar and essence together and beat until smooth and creamy. Spread over the cake and use a fork to give a rough-ened effect. Sprinkle the frosting with chopped walnuts and cut into squares.

Dairy Products

MILK

Fresh milk is an extremely versatile and nutritious food. It is natural, with no additives, colourings or preservatives. Milk provides not only protein but also a range of vitamins, and is the major source of dietary calcium for most people in Northern Ireland.

Calcium is essential throughout life to enable bones to grow, develop and remain strong and healthy. Lack of adequate amounts of dietary calcium can result in osteoporosis.

Grades of Milk Available in Northern Ireland

Milk is classified according to the heat treatment it receives and its butterfat content.

1. Wholemilk – (Silvertop) – Wholemilk has a fat content of 3.9% and is especially recommended for children under 5 years.

2. Semi-Skimmed Milk – (Red/Silver Striped) – Contains 1.8% fat.

3. Skimmed Milk – (Blue/ Silver Striped) – Contains 0.1% fat – is unsuitable for babies and not recommended for young children who need high energy foods.

4. Buttermilk – (Red/Silver patterned) – A cultured skimmed milk which contains 0.1% fat.

5. Heat Treatment – Either pasteurised or UHT (Ultra Heat Treated). UHT is a more severe heat treatment, and, therefore, the milk has a longer shelf life. Untreated milk (green top) is available. This milk, which is not heat treated, is bottled on the farm.

Care of Milk

It is important to remember that fresh, pasteurised milk is a perishable item so proper storage is necessary.

Take milk indoors as soon as it is delivered. Do not leave it in direct sunlight. Store in the refrigerator, preferably in the bottle in which it is delivered, for this has been sterilised before being filled.

THE NUTRITIONAL VALUE OF MILK

Per 284 ml (½ pt)	Energy		Protein (g)	Fat (g)	CHO (g)	Calcium (mg)	Vitamins
	K Cals	Kj					
Wholemilk	193	808	9.4	11.1	13.5	337	A,B,D,E
Semi-Skimmed	135	565	9.7	5.1	13.8	346	A,B,D,E
Skimmed	97	406	9.7	0.3	14.1	353	B
Buttermilk	87	364	9.7	0.3	12.2	346	B

Per 100 ml (3½ fl oz)	Energy		Protein (g)	Fat (g)	CHO (g)	Calcium (mg)	Vitamins
	K Cals	Kj					
Wholemilk	68	283	3.3	3.9	4.7	118	A,B,D,E
Semi-Skimmed	48	203	3.4	1.8	4.9	120	A,B,D,E
Skimmed	34	146	3.4	0.1	5.0	122	B
Buttermilk	31	130	3.4	0.1	4.3	122	B

FRESH DAIRY CREAM

Fresh dairy cream adds a luxurious feel to everyday meals, and, of course, it is ideal for entertaining. Fresh dairy cream is given heat treatments similar to milk.

Types of Fresh Dairy Cream

1) Whipping Cream – This type of fresh dairy cream has a minimum butterfat content of 35%. It is the most versatile and most widely used cream; e.g. fresh or tinned fruit, cereals, soups, sauces, casseroles and desserts.

2) Double Cream – This fresh dairy cream has a minimum butterfat content of 48%. It is deliciously rich, and can be used as a topping on soup or coffee and for piping on cakes or desserts.

3) Soured Cream – Made from whipping cream this product is extremely versatile and is superb in casseroles, salad dressings and cheesecakes. Butterfat content – same as whipping cream. Not suitable for freezing.

4) UHT Whipping Cream – This type of cream has a butterfat content similar to fresh whipping cream but receives a more severe heat treatment to give it a longer shelf life. Once opened, treat and use in the same way as fresh dairy cream.

Storing Fresh Dairy Cream – Check the date stamp before purchase to allow enough shelf life before use. Place the carton of cream in the refrigerator as soon as possible after purchase. Once opened, any unused cream should be kept in the carton and covered with a lid or cling film.

Freezing Fresh Dairy Cream – The best results are obtained by lightly whipping the cream before freezing and thawing for 24 hours in a refrigerator. The semi-whipped cream may then be whipped to the desired consistency after thawing. Alternatively pipe rosettes of cream, open freeze and pack in a rigid container. Storage time for whipping cream – up to two months; double cream – up to one month.

Whipping and Piping Cream

1. Start with a well chilled bowl and cold, fresh cream. Using either a balloon or a rotary whisk, quickly whip the cream, until a matt finish is reached. Continue more slowly and carefully until the cream stands in peaks on top of the whisk. The cream is now whipped.
2. To pipe whipped cream, use a piping bag and a star nozzle. Place the bag, with the nozzle, over a grater or tall glass to hold it in place while filling the bag with the whipped cream.
3. Remove and gently force the cream into the end of the bag. Twist the bag from the top.
4. Hold the piping bag at the end above the cream – and you are ready to pipe stars or rosettes. Any extra cream can be piped onto a baking tray, frozen, and stored for use later. This is a handy standby for decorating a trifle or sponge.

THE NUTRITIONAL VALUE OF FRESH DAIRY CREAM

Fresh Dairy Cream (per 100 ml)	Energy		Protein (g)	Fat (g)	CHO (g)	Calcium (mg)	Vitamins
	k cals	kJ					
Whipping Cream	336	1385	2.1	35	3.2	65	A,B,D,E
Double Cream	442	1819	1.7	48	2.6	49	A,B,D,E

CHEESE

Cheese is an excellent food for all of the family and can be given to babies from the age of nine months. It is very versatile, being ideal in cooking, salads, sandwiches, and on a cheese board.

Storage of Cheese

Store cheese either in a refrigerator or a cool larder at a temperature of 45°–55°F (8°–12°C). Wrap in aluminium foil or cling film and place in a container with a tightly fitting lid. To appreciate the full flavour and texture of cheese at its best, remove from the refrigerator or larder approximately one hour before use, so that it is at room temperature when served.

Freezing

The recommended storage time is three months for the more mature cheeses, without any deterioration of flavour.

Cheese does not freeze well in block form as it dries out and becomes very crumbly, making slicing impractical. For best results with cheddar type cheeses, grate and place in freezer bags, seal and freeze. To defrost, place in refrigerator for 24 hours before use.

Cottage Cheese

Cottage Cheese is a low fat, high protein food. It is extremely versatile and can be used for pâtés, moussakas, quiches, salads, cheese boards, party dips and cheesecakes.

Storage

Check the sell-by date before purchase and store in the refrigerator. After use always ensure that the carton is sealed, either with a lid or cling film.

Varieties of Cottage Cheese

Available as natural, or with added chives or chopped pineapple.

Varieties of Cheese

An increasing range of cheese varieties is made in Northern Ireland, including –

1. Double Gloucester
2. Leicester
3. Cheshire
4. Caerphilly
5. Wensleydale
6. Mild White Cheddar
7. Red Cheddar
8. Mature Cheddar
9. Low-Fat Cheddar
10. Vegetarian Cheddar
11. Smoked Cheddar
12. Varieties of Blended Cheddar Cheeses
13. Varieties of Blended Double Gloucester Cheeses
14. Varieties of Blended Red Leicester Cheeses
15. Mozzarella Cheese
16. Varieties of Cottage Cheeses
17. Varieties of Dessert Cheeses
18. Blue Veined, White Mould Cheese
19. Naturally Smoked Soft Cheese
20. Processed Cheese

THE NUTRITIONAL VALUE OF CHEESE

Cheese (Per 100 g)	Energy		Protein (g)	Fat (g)	CHO (g)	Calcium (mg)	Vitamins
	k cals	kJ					
Cheddar	412	1708	25.5	34.4	0.1	740	A,B,D,E
Low-Fat Cheddar	279	1167	30.9	17.2	Tr	897	A,B,D,E
Natural Cottage Cheese	95	398	12.5	4.1	2	80	A,B,D

BUTTER

Butter is made from cow's milk and is, therefore, a natural food, free from artificial preservatives, and cannot be matched for flavour and richness. It is unbeatable in baking and gives character and body to soups and sauces.

Butter has been eaten and enjoyed by people all over the world for at least 4,000 years. After all these years, it is still made essentially the same way – by churning fresh dairy cream. It takes the cream from 10.25 litres (18 pints) of milk to make a 450 g (1 lb) of butter.

Butter contains vitamins A, D and E and a small amount of protein. Both butter and margarine contain 80% fat.

THE NUTRITIONAL VALUE OF BUTTER

Butter (Per 100 g)	Energy		Protein (g)	Fat (g)	CHO (g)	Calcium (mg)	Vitamins
	k cal	kJ					
	733	3014	0.5	81	0.5	15	A,D,E

YOGURT

Yogurt is a cultured milk product which originated amongst the nomadic tribes of Eastern Europe. As well as being a refreshing snack or dessert, it enhances the flavour of both sweet and savoury dishes.

Storage – Always check the date stamp before purchase. Store in the refrigerator.

THE NUTRITIONAL VALUE OF YOGURT

Yogurt (Per 100 g)	Energy		Protein (g)	Fat (g)	CHO (g)	Calcium (mg)	Vitamins
	k cal	kJ					
Low-Fat Natural	61	275	6	1	7	180	A,B,E
Low-Fat Fruit	91	388	5	1	16	180	A,B,E
Very Low-Fat Fruit	40	173	4.5	0.1	5.5	150	A,B,E

Hilltown, Co. Down

Cookery Tips

1) Stir-fry soup vegetables in butter before adding stock for a better flavour.

2) A tablespoon of cream, added at the end of the cooking time makes a richer soup.

3) Soups, particularly vegetable soups taste better the day after making.

4) Grated cheddar cheese is a good accompaniment to vegetable soups.

5) Vegetable and pulse soups freeze well. If cream or a liaison of egg and cream is to be added, add when soup is thawed and re-heated.

6) To re-crisp a crusty loaf, wrap in foil and bake at 425°F, 220°C, Mark 7, for a few minutes.

7) To prevent dark rings forming around egg yolks, place in boiling water, lower the heat and simmer for 11 minutes. Drain eggs as soon as cooked, crack shells, cover with cold water, and leave until cold.

8) Crunchy topping – mix together equal parts of white or brown breadcrumbs and cheese, sprinkle it over the dish and place under the grill until browned.

9) A little paprika pepper sprinkled on cheese before grilling gives a lovely brown colour.

10) Bacon and parsley can be chopped quickly and easily with a pair of kitchen scissors.

11) Dry vermouth can be used as an alternative to wine in a recipe. Dilute it with an equal quantity of water. Especially good for fish and chicken

103

dishes.

12) Infuse milk with a bay leaf or onion when making a white sauce for a subtle flavour.

13) Sauces and custards to be prepared and used later in a recipe, should be poured into a bowl and covered with a circle of wetted greaseproof paper, to prevent a skin forming.

14) To skin a tomato, place it in boiling water for one minute, plunge into cold water and peel away the soft skin.

15) For perfectly cooked patna rice, first rinse rice under cold water, then place in pan full of boiling, salted water. Boil rapidly for 15 minutes until tender but not mushy. Place in a sieve and rinse with boiling water. Can be fluffed up for serving with an oiled fork.

16) When re-heating rice, place it in a saucepan with a few tablespoons of water and re-heat gently.

17) A mixture of mayonnaise and natural yogurt provides a light salad dressing.

18) Rinse wooden salad bowls in lukewarm water and dry thoroughly or wipe with absorbent paper. Never leave to soak in water.

19) Coat slices of apple, pear and banana in lemon juice in order to prevent discolouration.

20) Most mousses have a better flavour if allowed to stand at room temperature for about one hour before serving.

21) When crushing biscuits for a flan or cheesecake, place in polythene bag, tightly close and crush with a rolling pin.

22) To skin hazelnuts easily, place on a baking sheet, lightly toast for 2 to 3 minutes, transfer to a clean tea towel and gently rub off skins.

23) To make sure fresh Dairy Cream floats on top of Irish Coffee, pour it over the back of a teaspoon.

24) Buttercream keeps well for up to 3 weeks covered in the refrigerator.

25) Mix left over lemon or orange rind with caster sugar. Use for flavouring Victoria sandwich cakes.

26) Store cakes in an airtight tin. Wrap rich fruit cakes in greaseproof paper and then aluminium foil.

27) Do not place biscuits and cake in the same tin or the biscuits will absorb moisture and soften.

28) For softer scones, sprinkle baking tray and scones with plain flour before baking.

29) Wrap tea-breads in aluminium foil and they will last for approximately one week.

Dairy Products in your Microwave Oven

Microwave cookery is very different in many ways from cooking with a conventional cooker. It is versatile, economical, fast and easy to use. A microwave oven can cook fresh food, thaw frozen foods, and reheat already cooked food.

Food cooks very rapidly, so it is always safer to undercook and then return it again, after standing time. When food is removed from the microwave oven it continues to cook through from the heat generated within itself. Standing time allows for this, so it is very important to complete the cooking.

The timings given are for a 650 watt model, if you have a 500 watt model, then add 15 seconds longer for each minute. However, follow the instruction manual for your particular model and experiment with traditional recipes to give variety to your cooking.

Porridge

25 g (1 oz) porridge oats
426 ml (¾ pt) NI Milk
salt

Blend porridge oats and milk in a bowl, add a little salt. Do not cover. Microwave on high for 4-5 minutes, stirring after 2 minutes. Stir and serve.

White Sauce

25 g (1 oz) NI Butter
25 g (1 oz) plain flour
284 ml (½ pt) NI Milk
seasoning

Place butter in a microwave jug. Microwave on high for 30 seconds. Stir in flour, then gradually add milk. Microwave on high for 4 minutes, stirring every minute. Season.

Custard Sauce

284 ml (½ pt) NI Milk
15 ml (1 tbsp) sugar
15 ml (1 tbsp) custard powder
few drops vanilla essence

In a microwave jug, blend custard powder with a little cold milk, then pour in the remainder of milk; add sugar and vanilla essence. Microwave on high for 3 minutes, stirring briskly every minute.

Tips

Fresh Milk
1. Warm milk for drinks in the cups, and stir in flavourings.

2. Sauces and custards made in the jug cut down on washing up.

3. To prevent milk boiling over when cooking soups and sauces, use a container large enough to take twice the amount of liquid.

4. Egg custards can be cooked on low power if the container is placed in a dish of water.

5. Brush fish with milk for juicy flesh.

Cheese
1. When cooking cheese, it takes seconds not minutes.

2. For a quick Cheese Fondue put all the ingredients into a microwave proof dish, stir frequently. Allow 7–8 minutes on high for 450 g (1 lb) cheese.

Fresh Dairy Cream
1. In general stir cream into the dish after it has cooked. When the cream is folded in, as with quiches and soufflés, it can be cooked successfully on a low power.

Butter
1. Soften butter on low power for sandwich making – it makes the butter go further. Allow one minute for 225 g (8 oz). Remember to remove any foil wrapping and place butter on a plate.

2. Oil baking trays with melted butter.

ALSO . . .

Yeast Dough Base – Pizza
Microwaving can at least halve the time for proving
For 225 g (8 oz) quantity of flour place the dough in a bowl, cover with cling film. Prove by heating for 10 seconds and leaving to stand for 5 minutes. Repeat 2–3 times until it has doubled in size.

Vegetables
Virtually any fresh vegetables can be cooked in a microwave oven, and they remain crisp and colourful. As only a little water is needed, the water soluble vitamins are not lost in the cooking water. Salt should not be sprinkled directly on to the vegetables before cooking, as this can result in dehydration and toughness. Frozen vegetables cook quickly too, with no water needed as the melting ice serves this purpose.

DRYING HERBS

Herbs can be dried very successfully in a microwave oven. If possible pick clean, dry herbs, otherwise wash them thoroughly and pat dry with absorbent kitchen paper. Lay them out between layers of absorbent kitchen paper. Heat on high for 4–6 minutes. Check after the minimum time. When dry, the herbs will be brittle and crumble easily. Leave to cool before crushing and store in an airtight jar.

Index:

A Fresh Touch of *Natural Goodness,*